Hands Off! He's Mine

Hands Off! He's Mine

Debra McCormick

XULON ELITE

Xulon Press Elite
2301 Lucien Way #415
Maitland, FL 32751
407.339.4217
www.xulonpress.com

Due to the changing nature of the Internet, if there are any web addresses,
links, or URLs included in this manuscript, these may have been altered
and may no longer be accessible. The views and opinions shared in this
book belong solely to the author and do not necessarily reflect those of the
publisher. The publisher therefore disclaims responsibility for the views or
opinions expressed within the work.

Paperback ISBN-13: 978-1-6628-7258-7
Ebook ISBN-13: 978-1-6628-7259-4

Table of Contents

Chapter 1   Hands Off! He's Mine 9

Chapter 2   The Wedding Day 20

Chapter 3   Who Is This Man (Jekyll or Hyde)?................. 27

Chapter 4   Watch Out for All the Curves 33

Chapter 5   Let's Go All the Way to the Top 46

Chapter 6   A Week in a Country Jail........................... 52

Chapter 7   Help! There's No Way Out! 57

Chapter 8   Breaker, Breaker, What's Your Handle? 69

Chapter 9   Ride of Terror................................... 76

Chapter 10   Two Dozen Yellow Roses 79

Chapter 11   Where the Deer and the Roaches Will Play 83

Chapter 12   Pregnant Again 87

Chapter 13   Disaster Strikes................................ 92

Chapter 14   Trick or Treat, Kick Him with My Feet 97

Chapter 15   What's Growing in the Window? 104

Chapter 16   Standoff at Conrad 107

Chapter 17   The Hideout 117

Chapter 18   The Final Curtain Must Come Down.............. 121

"Hands Off! He's mine," I exclaimed as my older sister, Kathy, and I peeked through our bedroom door. We were busy watching my mom talking with her cousin, whom she hadn't seen in years. I was referring to a friend her cousin had brought with him. They had traveled from Kentucky to Phoenix and had decided to swing by and visit my mom.

This particular friend of his bore a powerful resemblance to Elvis. He had dark hair and flawless blue eyes that pierced right through me with an unforgettable glare. He had long, shadowy sideburns and even wore a V-neck velour silver shirt that seemed to fit him just right.

"Do you suppose he even sings like Elvis,?" I wondered as I gazed at him. "Oh well, close enough." It was love at first sight.

These are the words that still ring deep within my ears as I wonder why I made the choices I did at only fifteen; now desiring to go back and live my life for Jesus, changing the wrong choices into the right choices ones, as the Lord, had planned for me.

How could the next seventeen years of my life go so wrong when I had lived my life for Jesus? I had come from a Christian home, never involving myself in sinful behavior. Or was that an outrageous, erroneous statement to make?

The journey you are about to embark upon is that of a peculiar, unconventional lifestyle, yet amazingly similar to others, but it is my story. In reading this story, I hope that lives can be forever changed by seeing that God wants us to ask Him what He thinks about the relationships we get into.

As I reminisce on something that was so wrong, I see how it was used to bring glory to my God and Savior through the testimony of truth.

To God I give the honor and the glory for allowing me to share part of my life's testimony, which includes the good, the bad, and the ugly, yet it all molded me into the Christian woman I am today.

God has a plan for each of us, plans to prosper us and not harm us, plans to give us hope and a future (Jer. 29:11). But so many times, we chose our own paths and make many wrong turns.

Introduction

For you to understand this story, I must tell you about my upbringing. There was my mom, who was the spiritual backbone of my family. She was very strong in the Lord and a very strict mom. She shielded her children from the world but taught us the love of God. I always saw her giving but not receiving. She was a kindhearted woman and very pretty, looking much younger than her years.

I always remember people coming to our home and my mom fixing big meals, sometimes for fifty or more. Wow, was she a good cook. She could make water biscuits and water gravy that would melt in your mouth. She was the kind of cook who could make something to eat even when it looked like there was nothing.

Mom, also had another gift the Lord had given her, and that was her writing ability that made people laugh. She wrote everything from love songs to songs about Christ, His life, and His love. But strangely, she never took the time to publish them, for she thought God wouldn't be pleased.

We did manage to go into ministry by singing my mom's songs, church by church, in many states, as well as Canada and Mexico. We went whenever we were asked. Oh! You are probably wondering who the "we" was. Well, the "we" consisted of my mom, who sang lead, along with my older sister, singing a high harmony, and myself, singing alto.

I can tell you I know now God blessed me with a singing voice, which started to shine at age three. Our group was called the "Jackson Trio," and we only sang in Baptist churches. I do remember where ever we went; people loved the harmonies and said they were blessed.

I lived my life through the legacy of my grandfather, who was a great preacher, as well as my dad and my uncle. So, of course, as a child, I loved being in ministry, not because I loved the Lord, but because I loved to sing.

Now back to the rest of my family. There was my dad, who preached for many years as well as being a missionary, but suddenly stopped and never told any of us why, and we never asked.

Growing up, I never remember my dad and my mom being very close, and in time, he left and got married again. He was never physically abusive to us children but was to my mom. I also didn't realize that most of his communication with us was through screaming, which took a toll on us as children, but it was his only way of communicating.

My dad left when I was seventeen, but I don't remember missing him, and I can't even remember him hugging me, but he did come to my wedding and gave me away. I guess you can say missing him finally caught up with me when I attended his funeral. I was very angry at him as I looked at him in his coffin, but then I began to cry and told him I loved him and forgave him. I guess I did miss him.

The rest of my family consisted of two brothers and three sisters, myself being the middle child of five until my youngest brother was born, which was by my stepfather.

My years of childhood were mostly good ones; there were so many fond memories, very few sad, and many funny ones. Let me share a few of them so you can understand my life better and why things happened the way they did.

My mom was a comedian at heart, for we never knew what she was going to do, and my dad was a man who had no shame whatsoever. Believe me, the two of them together was a story in itself.

My dad would do things, and it seemed to me he really didn't think about what he was saying or doing before doing them. If he saw a sign that said to stay off the grass, he had to walk on it.

At age ten, my parents, had met a man named Lee, who was going to our church and had become great friends with him. He was always talking about how California was and after living in Kentucky all their lives, decided to move us out to California. There were seven of us, mom, dad and five children plus Lee who was going to guide us there and we would stay with one of his sisters until we found a place of our own.

The year was 1964 when we left Kentucky for good. After packing two cars, off we went, singing, "California, here we come."

When we got to California, the first town we all wanted to see was Hollywood. Of course, Sunset Boulevard was the first stop on our agenda.

But wait! There's more to this story. Let me describe "how" we went down Sunset Boulevard. If you remember the show *The Beverly Hillbillies*, that would probably describe us the best. If you're a younger generation, look it up on Google, and then you'll understand.

Let me describe what we looked like. Our car was an old station wagon from the fifties. I believe it was light blue with a roof rack on top and packed pretty high. The car wasn't the problem; it was what followed behind the car. We pulled a homemade, and I mean *homemade*, customized, one-of-a-kind trailer that my dad, our friend and brother had built. The frame had been the back of an old pick-up truck and gray in color from the fifties. The men had built up with wood three sides to make it taller so it would hold all of our belongings.

Then at the back above the tailgate was a white door turned sideways that hung from two hinges. Even worse, on the outside of the trailer, on both sides, were doors (the kind that go in the front of a house) but positioned sideways, attached with hinges to the outside of the trailer. Then there were chains attached to the top of the trailer that was attached to the doors so when letting them down, they became beds or could be used as tables.

At night, we had two thin mattresses that fit on each door so that two of us could sleep comfortable. In the daytime, we would fold them back up against the trailer sides, and the mattresses were placed inside the trailer.

Now you can imagine, to a ten-year-old, this would have been pretty embarrassing even in 1964. Also, there was my 13 year old sister and 14 year old brother. They were probably more embarrassed than me.

Again, things looked even worse. On the front of this trailer (yes, on the outside), my dad had nailed my little brother's tricycle along with some of

5

Mom's black iron skillets in clear view for everybody to see. Hopefully, you get the picture, and we will move on with the story.

As we drove down Sunset Blvd, my mom turned around to say something to one of us when a shocking discovery caught her eyes that made her start screaming at my dad. "Bill Jackson, what have you done now? I swear you have no pride whatsoever." (I told you he didn't have any pride.) By this time, we had all looked out the back window and decided it was better if we rode on the floorboard of the car.

What we didn't know was that while we were at the last stop, my dad had taken ropes and tied one end to the front of the trailer on both sides and the other end to the back of the rack on top of our car. And swinging happily on the ropes was my youngest brother's diapers, just flapping in the wind.

You can now imagine what we looked like. People were pointing and laughing at what they saw. They thought another part of the *Beverly Hillbillies* had  come to town; all we lacked was Granny's rocking chair.

If it had been today, there would be a good chance phones would have been clicking, and we would have been posted on Facebook, Twitter, or Snapchat.

Before finishing our tour, we made a stop, and Mom took down the diapers (they were dry), and we started back on our way.

After finishing a few days of sightseeing, we settled in a city called Riverside, at least for a few months. It seemed like we moved every wash day. We attended two to four schools a year and always somehow adjusted but never put down any solid roots. I remember we were all above-average students and did very well in school despite our strange circumstances.

We also went from church to church. My mom was very picky and couldn't find a church like the one we had attended in Kentucky. California churches were too liberal and, as quoted by her, "wishy, washy," and did not serve God but man.

At the time, I couldn't understand and thought, "How could every church be so wrong and Momma right?" But I knew not to ask, think, or go there.

Sometimes we tried two to three churches per Sunday, and all the ones we visited allowed the women to speak. A woman speaking in church was next to the biggest sin that could be committed. And we knew what the biggest sin was. It was the way women dressed and, as quoted by Momma, "God wouldn't step one foot in any of these churches, and neither will we."

Eventually, many years later after all my siblings and I had married and we had searched town by town and walking out of service by service, my mom decided we would start having services in our homes, which was directed by her. Throughout the process, my stepdad become the pastor and provided the preaching. If we went to sleep, my stepfather would squirt us with a plastic water gun he carried in his coat or placed in the pulpit. By now we all had children and they began to hate church, and so did I, at least ours.

I hope I have allowed you into a part of my childhood and early adult life to let you know we did not live a normal Christian life, but my life had a lot of happiness and fun in it because Momma made it that way. In no way am I putting my parents down, and I loved my mom very much. I thank her every day for teaching us God's Word to the best of her knowledge.

Let me share with you what a typical day was like for me.

I remember the time when my sister and I were teenagers and had two boys over from church. When we would see Mom disappear, we would worry, for we never knew what kind of stunt she would pull next. People who knew her called her Lucy with a different twist.

We were sitting in the living room talking when suddenly, the window began to open. We watched as one leg came in and then the rest of the body and, yes, you guessed who it was. As Mom entered the room, I could feel my face begin to turn red, and the boys sat speechless, not knowing how to react but sitting with their mouths hung wide open.

Here stood this grown woman dressed in blue gingham, short full-skirted dress (no one had ever seen my mom in a short dress), something like a square dancer wore in the fifties, and even had a white pinafore apron

7

over it. She had fixed her hair in two braids, with blue ribbons on the ends tied into bows. Now if you think that wasn't weird enough, she also had on a pair of glasses she had made out of a clothes hanger. And to finish off her ensemble, she had on bobby socks along with a pair of princess patent-style shoes and was chewing wildly on a big wad of bubble gum.

My mom slowly eased her way over to the arm of the couch where my sister's friend was sitting and slid down right next to him, placing one arm around his shoulders and the other pushing her hair glamorously up close to her forehead while she bent down, and in a sweet soft-tainted Southern accent, whispered, "How-day! I'm Melba, Kathy and Debbie's younger sister and the prettiest by far. I knows you don't know me cause they try to keep me hid, and I really don't know why, but I'm the smartest by far. How's about a date?"

By this time, the guys were falling off the couch with hysterical laughter, as well as my mom and sister. But I sat there, not laughing or crying. I think I was in shock, liking it, but not knowing how to let go and react. Mom always seemed to know how to break the ice for us. It was like she always knew how I felt. I'm sure she knew how bashful I was and was only trying to help besides just loving to have some fun. At this point, they had met our mom and were feeling right at home.

We moved from state to state so many times that I couldn't count, but we always ended back in Southern California. We were like a band of gypsies and didn't stop after I got married until the final curtain came down.

To this day, I am not much for moving. I have been in Southern California for almost fifty years or more at this writing and like to be grounded. These stories hopefully will help you to better understand the rest of this book.

CHAPTER 1

Hands Off! He's Mine

The year was 1968, and we were living in Phoenix, Arizona. I had just quit the tenth grade and was fifteen years old. There was so much going on that I didn't understand or couldn't cope with. It was a time when free love was in and marijuana and other drugs were sold openly in the schools along with micro miniskirts and paper dresses.

I felt like I was the only one in the whole wide world who dressed and lived my kind of lifestyle, and I felt very out of place. School consisted of me having no friends, and even the ones who said they were Christians didn't mingle with me, and I wondered why. Why were we so different?

I never felt like I could talk with Momma or my older sister until years later when I found out my sister felt the same way. Talking wasn't a thing we did in our house, at least if the subjects were about boys, sex, or sins.

We were taught that any secular fun was sin. I remember longing to go watch a movie, visit an amusement park, attend a nice party, go bowling, and so on, but everything was wrong. I felt very alone as a result. I knew I loved God, well, sort of, but I wanted to do some of the things the other kids did, but everything that seemed to be fun was "wrong."

Because we lived a very strict lifestyle and Mom never budged on any issue, whether it was about what we could wear or do, it was sin, and there was no discussion. I didn't want to wear micro miniskirts, but I wanted to fit in a little, maybe a skirt just above the knees. I remember we wore dresses one or two inches below the knees, and I would roll my skirt up when I left the house just to fit in, then when starting home, I'd let it back down again. Mama just couldn't understand some things, and I couldn't talk to her about how I felt. Her rules were set in stone and hard to follow, so I just tried to stick with them as much as possible.

The day was a sunny, warm Sunday afternoon, and we had just gotten home from church. Mom was cooking dinner in the kitchen, and I was in the living room watching TV. Suddenly, there was a knock at the front door. As I opened the door, a young man I guessed to be about twenty-five years old, blond, and approximately 5'7" stood on the other side. He asked me if this was where Gladys Jackson lived; he said she was his aunt.

Before I knew it, I had shut the door in his face and ran to the kitchen with excitement and told Mom, "Mom, there's a man at the door who says he's your nephew. His name is James Martin."

Seeing someone we knew was very rare, especially family. We had left all family behind in Kentucky on both my mom and dad's side to start over out west. Mom didn't wait to reply but ran out of the kitchen and opened up the front door. She apologized for my shutting the door in his face as they both embraced each other. She said she hadn't seen him for over fourteen years so having a visitor and especially being family was a very exciting time.

As I sat and listened, James told my mom how he was at his mom's house when a set of saltshakers came in the mail that my mom had sent her as a souvenir from California. At the time, he and two of his friends were packed to vacation out west (mainly old Mexico), where he said it was "to live it up a little" and told his mom he'd look my mom up while they were here.

Then my mom said, "You mean you have somebody else with you?"

"Oh yes. They're out in the car. They don't feel too well."

What he didn't tell us was that they were hungover from partying in old Mexico the night before. Of course, Mom insisted on him bringing them in.

At this point, I left the room and went to my bedroom to share the good news with my older sister Kathy. By this time, the two other guys were in the house. We opened the door just enough to peek out and see what they looked like. At my first glance at one of them, I said to my sister, "Hands off! He's mine," not knowing that phrase would be the turning point in my life that would haunt me for the rest of my life.

As time passed, my sister and I moseyed out of our bedroom to the living room, where Mom and James were talking. I sat and listened but occasionally glanced over at one of his friends and smiled as he smiled back. I couldn't get over how good-looking he was. I noticed he was very quiet, a young man with dark brown hair and the brightest blue eyes that seemed to draw mine to his. His eyes always seemed to be looking back as well. Everyone in the room sat quietly as Mom and James talked about old times and reminisced on it all.

By now, the rest of the family had entered the room and joined in the conversation. My cousin had introduced his friends to all of us and said their names were John and Benny. John was the one whose eyes had met mine.

As we all sat around talking, Mom noticed that John had a headache and asked me to get him some water and aspirin, so, of course, I was more than glad to do it but yet very self-conscience of every step I took, scared he was watching me but at the same time wanting him to.

As I think back, I had a hard time talking with boys or even thinking they'd look at me. With the way we dressed and the lifestyle we lived, not many kids our age wanted to be friends with us very long. Or my mom quickly found fault with them after a few days, and we had to end our friendships. It was worse with girls than guys. Mom had this thing that none of our girlfriends could live up to her standards, so it left us empty-handed.

As I continued to listen, my cousin told us a very strange story. He said he was married, but his wife had left him and moved to Georgia. He had found out through his two children that his wife was living with two men. At that point, he and two of his friends had moved into an apartment together. Of course, he forgot to tell the part about the three girls who were living with them, which we found out later.

As he kept talking, he began to cry, and, of course, as always, Mom fell for the tears. When a chance opened up for witnessing about Jesus, Mom did. He told her he missed his wife and kids and wanted them to come home. Mom said, "Are you willing to forgive her for the wrong she's done? For the Lord wants to see you make it." As she witnessed to him about the Lord, he said he wanted to rededicate his life to the Lord. After praying together, his new journey began.

As my cousin's story continued, Mom asked him if he had the number for where his wife was (there were no cell phones back then). My mom had always loved to counsel people. She allowed James to call Georgia and talk with his wife. Then Mom got on the phone as well and talked with her for a time, finding out all the facts he had left out.

It was at that time that things began to move so fast. The next thing we knew, he was leaving his two friends with us and was taking my eighteen-year-old brother back to Georgia to pick up his wife and kids.

At this point, John spoke up and said, "What about Bennie and me?" By the way Bennie was the name of his other friend.

"Oh, you'll be okay," as he rushed out the door. "I'll be back in three days; Gladys will take good care of you."

I always wondered if Mom had time to make a decision or if she just let it happen. Well, no matter what, we had two new boarders.

The next few days were like a fairy tale that moved very fast. I had met my knight in shining armor, and I was the princess. How could a person be so kind and perfect in every way? To me, John was perfect in every way, even though I really didn't know anything about him but had fathomed a perfect man in my fifteen-year-old mind.

After knowing John for one week, I knew this was the man I wanted to spend the rest of my life with, and no one could take his place. John and I talked a lot about everything from bicycles to family and began to fall in love, or what I thought was love. At that moment, my life was complete, except he needed to propose to me. Would he, and did he feel the same way?

As I look back, why did my mom ever allow our relationship to progress? She was the mom, and I was the kid. She was supposed to protect me and know what was good for me. She was so strict with us, yet he was twenty-one, and I was only fifteen. What was she thinking?

One night we were sitting out front in two lounge chairs under the kitchen window, where the light shone through. Because I was so young, Mom made sure I stayed in sight and had to sit in the light. As we sat there talking, I suddenly heard the window break above our heads, and a head of cabbage came right over John's head, so he ducked. I knew what had happened and felt so embarrassed because my mom and dad were screaming at each other, which was nothing out of the ordinary. We decided it might be a good idea to get up and go inside. I think if that had not happened, he would have told me he liked me that night and maybe even snuck a kiss, but that came a little later.

The next day, my cousin got back with his wife and two children. After that, things seemed to progress rapidly in the next few days that followed. Suddenly, John wouldn't speak to me. It was like he was scared to. I didn't understand, but I became physically sick until my mom stepped in and asked, "What's wrong with you?" I explained how John had told me he liked me one night and then started ignoring me. To make things worse, he had started talking to my older sister and asked her out. This was bad because I was too young to date, but my sister was not, so I was very angry with my sister.

Not understanding, my mom went to John's room, which he was sharing with our friend, Lee, older brother, and his friend Benny. She confronted him, saying, "What is your problem?" His reply was that Lee had told him I was only fifteen and to back off, for my mom would never allow him to date a fifteen-year-old, but because my sister was already eighteen, he could date her. John explained that he thought I was the eighteen-year-old and Kathy the fifteen-year-old. He said James, Mom's cousin, had told him one of us was the oldest, and he assumed it was me because I didn't act fifteen.

At this point, Mom became very angry with Lee for speaking for her, which no one did. My mom ruled our house even though she taught us the man was the head of the family. "How dare you speak for me without asking me my opinion! How would you know what I would say?"

Then she looked at John and asked him, "How do you feel about Debbie? Did you know she was only fifteen?" (Remember, he was twenty-one.)

John said, "I really like her a lot. I've never met a girl quite like her, and no I didn't know she was only fifteen. I thought she was the oldest between her and her sister Kathy."

At that moment, Mom agreed we could go steady, but she would observe our relationship. If only my mom would have stepped in and said no, I believe I would have listened. But I believe out of spite of being the head, she chose not to.

That night, my cousin's wife asked if John could drive her to a department store. She also asked me to tag along. I found out later that she had asked me to go so we could be together without my mom watching me like a hawk. The sad thing: My mom consented.

While waiting in the car, as my cousin's wife went shopping, John kissed me for the first time. This was the very first kiss that I had consented to, and wow, was it a kiss! I had let a boy kiss me when I was eleven but didn't like it because he tried to French-kiss me. That was the end of that. I slapped him and gave up on kissing. But tonight was different. I was fifteen years old and knew what I was doing. I thought I was so mature, just like every fifteen-year-old, but I was no different.

This was the first time since then that I felt like I was ready to actually have a real boyfriend, but I felt like it was a lifelong commitment. Our relationship grew over the next few weeks, thinking he did no wrong.

Since John was living in our house, my mom and stepdad witnessed to him all the time because he was not a Christian. I admit that he not being a Christian bothered me because I loved the Lord, or at least I thought I did. But I knew being in my house meant that it was only a matter of time before he would be.

At our house, Mom made sure it was Bible in the morning, Bible in the noontime, and Bible at suppertime. (For those not from back east, that means dinner time). Of course, only after a couple of weeks of staying with us, John accepted the Lord. Everyone in the house was excited; there was no greater thrill than to see someone come to Jesus. Now that we were both Christians, I knew that one day we would live happily ever after.

As I look back, there were so many warning signs telling me to turn and go the other way, but my infatuation with him caused me to ignore every one of them.

Within the first three months of dating, John started getting quite a lot of mail from his grandmother, and, of course, my mother, "the wise detective," became suspicious. She showed me three letters that came the same day from his grandmother but told me to notice how the handwriting was different on all three envelopes and to smell the sweet aroma one of them had.

The next thing my mom did was get nosy and open the letters (at least that's what I thought at the time), whether she was wrong or right is neither here nor there, but she did it, trying to protect me and get me to change my mind and walk away. To my surprise (not hers), all three letters were from different girls, evidently his girlfriends from different areas. Here was this young man living in my home, eating my food, and saying he loved me. Did this stop the way I felt about him? Of course not, but it did scare me. I felt I must be doing something wrong and needed to change me. This would be my goal, to change into the person he wanted me to be. I thought John would walk away, but he didn't. He managed to have an explanation for everything, and I believed him.

As time went on, we left Phoenix and moved back to San Diego. Houses were scarce to find, so we stayed for a while on the outskirts of town in a pull-off road spot. We finally found a house nobody lived in, but neighbors said the owners were out of town. Mom said, "Let's just stay in the garage and start fixing up the house for the landlord, and maybe he'll let us live there."

Sure enough, we had already painted and cleaned up the house when the landlord came by. Mom explained our situation, and he let us stay there. God was good to us. He said the house looked great and gave us six months of free rent.

John got a job at a service station but kept working overtime a lot. We stopped by one night just to say hi, and they said John never worked overtime and was on a date with his girlfriend. They didn't know me, and I didn't tell them. When I confronted him, he convinced me they just lied to me.

After about a year, Mom got restless, and we left for Texas, and John moved with us. We settled in a little town called Knock-A-Nut, approximately sixty miles from San Antonio and ten miles to Seguin, the watermelon capital of the world.

We pulled our trailer (which was a real trailer) into the yard of this little church we started to attend. This was a community we were not accustomed to. The first day we were there, the ladies of the church brought us a home-cooked breakfast fit for a king, along with cold milk straight from the cow and bacon that I found out was deer. That I had to think about!

John and my brother looked for work, but jobs were scarce. One funny, story that stands out was when both of them got jobs in a chicken plucking plant. They left in the morning, and both quit by noon and walked home by way of a dried-up creek bed, which was nearly nine miles from our home. Neither was able to work because they couldn't stomach cleaning chickens. Finally, all the men of the house found jobs for minimum wage at a nearby feed mill.

As weeks passed, we settled into a house, then hunger set in. Believe me when I say we were hungry, I mean we were hungry, and that was no exaggeration. I remember one day we were hungry, and all the men had just started their jobs but had not been paid. Mom and us girls were at home trying to figure out what we would eat. Suddenly, my sister and I decided to go across the street and get a watermelon to eat. Mama said that when the disciples were hungry, the Lord let them get corn out of the corn fields. Now across the street was not corn but watermelons, and we were hungry. I think we had a small jar of peanut butter half full and one pack of crackers left in the house to feed eleven people for three more days until payday.

Remember, this was the watermelon capital of the world. The smallest watermelon looked like one of the biggest ones you could find in a grocery store or fruit stand. These were even bigger. Have you ever heard that everything is bigger in Texas? Well, believe it.

My sister and I decided we wouldn't starve, so we went to climb the fence and get us one. While climbing the fence, both of us eyed which one we would take. At the same time, we noticed storm clouds gathering, and it looked as if it would rain. Even the smallest watermelons were so large that we couldn't pick them up. We each began to roll one toward the house.

They were so heavy that we could only roll them a little at a time. Then the rain began to pour, so you can imagine how wet we were when we got back to the house with the watermelons. But we had a good laugh, and the watermelons sure tasted good to some hungry people.

After about three months, we were invited to sing at a conference down in Houston. We all went and stayed in a trailer outside the church. After the first morning meeting, John told me he had a headache and would lie down for a while till the second service. I knew at the time he seemed to act a little nervous, but the next services were ready to start, so I didn't think much more about it.

Later that night, when the services were over, we all went out to the trailer to retire for the evening. To my surprise, John was not in the trailer, but on his bunk was a letter explaining he had to leave to straighten out his life back home in Kentucky and would call us later. You'd think this would have ended my dream since I was only fifteen, and I would more than likely move on to explore other relationships, but no, not me. I was madly in love and thought I'd see him again one day because I knew he would miss me and come back.

After living in Texas for six months and things not seeming to get any better, Mom and Dad decided to move back to Kentucky. We pulled our trailer in the backyard of my Granny's house till we found a place and settled down there for a while.

Somehow John found us and gave my mom a call to say he was going out west to California to work on a job. He told her he wanted to stop by and just say hello before leaving. When he came by, my heart did flip-flops the whole time he was there, but I stayed in the other room and just looked out and listened, too shy to come out. As he was leaving, he asked if I was going to come out to say good-bye, so Mom came into the bedroom and got me. She didn't seem to understand how I was hurting or how I felt and told me I was acting foolish. She also told me if she was me, she'd be out there trying to stop him from leaving, but I couldn't. I couldn't understand why I was hurting, and how could I hurt so much? If only someone could have talked to me and explained to me why I was feeling as I did. I finally got the nerve to come out, and John hugged me good-bye and said he'd miss me and that he would write.

I still didn't start living a normal young girl's life, you know, having fun with other girls and liking other boys, the things that most teenage girls did. Instead my love for John worsened. All I could think of was him, day in and day out. I think Mom knew she had a problem on her hands but didn't know how to handle me. Here I was, now seventeen, and my love for John had grown stronger. I remember thinking, "Why does love have to hurt so much? Am I normal? Am I like every other girl my age?" I wish I could have talked with someone, but I kept everything inside. Mom tried, but I could not tell her how I felt. I didn't think she'd understand. Looking back, she would have, but I was scared she'd tell me what I did not what to hear. I chose to keep everything inside. I remember thinking nobody really understood what I was going through.

After months of agony, I finally received a letter from John. In the letter, he stated he had thought about me day and night and wanted to come back to Kentucky and have me by his side for the rest of his life. I fathomed at this point he had been going through the same things I had been going through, and as I read on, his letter touched my soul and eased my heart once again. He continued on by stating that when he got back, he wanted to stop by and see me and discuss our future together if I wanted it. He said his hope and prayer was that we'd spend the rest of our lives together and never be apart again. My world came alive once again at that point. His last sentence was that he had something for me.

It seemed as if my life lit up; he was coming back, and my prayers had been answered. The next couple of weeks passed so slowly, but then came the night John pulled up in front of my house. Somebody dropped him off, and he came inside and greeted everybody and chatted with the family till late in the night. Eventually, things died down, and most of the family went to bed. Mom said I could go outside on the front porch and talk with him.

As we sat outside, John told me how he had thought of nothing else but me for the last one and a half years. As we sat beside each other, he eased out of his chair to a kneeling position in front of me, continuing to tell of his love for me while reaching into his pocket to pull out a little envelope. My heart was pounding to the beat of many drums, and in an instant, he said, "Debbie, will you marry me?"

Suddenly, all of heaven seemed to race through my head, and I looked at him with my eyes all aglow while his arms began to embrace me. Then I said, "Yes, yes, yes!" I felt this was the happiest day in my life.

John slid the engagement ring on my finger with pride and smiled and said, "I love you and will never leave you."

As I broke the news to my family, the excitement seemed to stop with me. I just couldn't understand why. Why weren't they as happy as I was? Why couldn't they rejoice with me? But no matter what, my joy would flow on. Nobody would take that from me.

For the next few weeks, my mom tried to talk to me, but I guess you could say I never listened. I remember one of the things she said to me was, "You mark my words, in a few years, you'll have a lot of kids, and he'll leave you all alone." She told me, "You're living a dream, but your dream is going to turn into a nightmare." I thought she just hated John and didn't want me to be happy.

How foolish we are as children to not realize that our parents are more intelligent than we are. Usually, they know just a little bit more than we do, especially if they are filled with the Holy Spirit. Now that I'm a mother and have gone through some challenges of my own, I've asked myself why my mother didn't step in and just say, "No, you will not marry him," but she didn't. I asked her once, and she told me she knew I wouldn't listen and didn't want me to run away because I had just turned seventeen. But I don't think I would have.

How about you? Where are you at right now? Are you in a similar position? If you are a Christian, please listen to that still, soft voice within your soul (the Holy Spirit) and listen to your parents, grandparents, pastors, teachers, and good friends; just listen. And if you aren't a Christian, talk to somebody and get out while you can.

CHAPTER 2

The Wedding Day

The next few weeks passed by quickly as I awaited the dream of my life. We needed to shop for the invitations and my dress. Oh how the excitement grew. There was so much to do: make the guest list, plan the reception, match the colors and pick the dresses for the bridesmaids. Since Christmas was just a few weeks away, I decided my colors for the wedding would be red.

The wedding would be at our house, and I would come down the spiral staircase. We lived in a two-story house that was decorated in the early 1900s style. The decor in all the rooms was gold and red. We had a parlor room where the staircase was located as well as two big sliding doors that went into the formal living room. That room connected to another set of sliding doors that went into our formal dining room, where a long, beautiful table with twelve red satin upholstered chairs and matching hutch rested.

This would be a beautiful setting for a wedding, maybe close to *Gone with the Wind*. It felt even more like a fairy tale, just another chapter in my fantasy world. Maybe I had watched too many love stories on TV. Was love *A Many-Splendored Thing*? Would my dream ever become a reality? Time would tell. In this day and time, it could have been a reality story.

My sister and I took our first bus ride to downtown Lexington by ourselves. We were filled with excitement, knowing we were shopping for my wedding dress. My sister never said much about the wedding except she didn't feel that he really loved me and that she thought I was making the biggest mistake of my life, but on this day, she didn't bring anything up; she just joined in with my excitement. My sister and I were very close, and she realized that once I got married, we could never be as close as we were before.

The room I shared with my sister was beautiful. It was the only bedroom downstairs. The entrance went out from under the staircase located in the parlor. We also had our own bathroom, which included a bear claw tub that we had painted hot pink with a flower decal on it. The whole bathroom was decorated in hot pink and black.

The bedroom had an alcove where a gold-fringed floor lamp stood between two antiqued wine-velvet chairs. Each week our allowances bought something to decorate our little apartment, as we called it. It was our private place, where we enjoyed staying up all night laughing and being in each other's company. Life was so simply, and I had no worries.

My sister had done all the decorating, for when it came to designing, I was the world's worst, so I just helped her. Yet now she was willing to sacrifice her room (her hard work) for me. John and I would be taking the room because we couldn't afford a place of our own. That should have told me we weren't ready. I realize now how selfish I was, for I only thought of John and myself.

I knew Mom only had a limited amount of money because she and Dad had separated, even though they still lived in the same house. He stayed gone more than he was home. But these things would not stop my world from turning, for I would marry Prince Charming, and we would live happily ever after. My marriage would not end up like Mom and Dad's. John loved me and said he would never leave me. I believed him, and that was that.

Now back to the ride on the bus. We went to a little shop that was going out of business and sold wedding gowns. Money was tight, but I knew how to be conservative and picked out a beautiful, beaded gown with a long train but at a price Mom could afford. I could just imagine how Cinderella felt when she tried on the beautiful ball gown. If only I could wear this gown forever. We paid down on the gown and veil and continued to a shop that sold wedding invitations. Then it was on to a fabric shop where my sister picked out all the material to make her dress and my sisters'. She was good at designing and came up with beautiful gowns that looked like they were made for princesses. Finally, everything was finished. We went home very tired but full of excitement.

We invited family and friends on my side, but when it came to John's, he didn't want to invite anyone. He stated his family was not to be invited and told of many tales regarding his mom and how she had treated him growing up. He lived with his dad from the time he was fifteen, and at age seventeen, his dad committed suicide, so the reports said, but he told us that his father's family had assumed his mother had somehow had a hand in it.

Nevertheless, I didn't persist when it came to invitations but respected his wishes and never brought the subject up again. At that moment, I realized I didn't know anything about John's past or family except what little he had told me, which were various bizarre stories, but he was my Prince Charming, and I knew he was perfect and one of a kind. I definitely would not let anything ruin our wedding.

We arraigned an interview with a pastor my mom knew well and sat down with him and went through all the plans. He counseled us on what marriage presented and how Christ should be the center of our lives. John answered all the questions right, and I just knew we were ready. I also knew I was marrying a man who loved God. Time moved rapidly for the first time since we had been apart.

Back at the house, the next two weeks were busy; making sure everything was clean as well as touch-ups on painting. In the dining room, there was a beautiful cherry table that seated twelve people nicely. On it laid a gorgeous red linen tablecloth that had been placed on the table with clear plastic to protect it. This was where my four-tiered cake with red roses on each layer would be placed. The stairwell was lined with white streamers and big red bows. The streamers hung in loops, with the bows at the top of each loop. The preparation lasted till everything was in place, down to the last corner being cleaned. The house had never looked so beautiful. Everyone had given their all. Finally, everything was complete.

That night, I didn't sleep much, thinking of the big day ahead of me. As morning peeked through the windows, I knew the big day had arrived. I jumped up and took a shower and rolled my hair, thinking of nothing except that by 8 p.m., I would no longer be Debra Jackson but Debra Henry. How would I feel? Would I look different? Would I finally be a woman?

My storybook romance would end happily ever after, and I would get the man of my dreams.

The whole house seemed to be full of excitement that morning despite all the negative thoughts that existed. Even Mom had put away her fears; at least it seemed that way at the moment. The day seemed to pass very slowly, but eventually, 5 p.m. came. I started to prepare myself for the big step.

My dad arrived, and Mom said we needed to go to the store to buy the sherbet and the 7 Up for the punch because she hadn't bought enough. My dad said he would go if someone would go in, so I thought it couldn't take but a few minutes and volunteered to go. After coming out of the store, Dad tried to start the car, but it wouldn't start.

Oh great, now what was I going to do? Here I was supposed to be getting ready in thirty minutes, but I was stuck outside the store with curlers in my hair and the sherbet melting.

Dad went to the phone booth and called someone, I don't remember who, and I really don't remember who came; all I remember is by the time I got home, guests were already arriving, and I had to try to sneak pass them and run up the steps to get ready.

The bathroom I got ready in was something out of a storybook. The room was a twelve by twelve with plush dark blue carpet, a big bear claw tub, and even an old-fashioned dressing table, the kind you'd see in a romance movie.

My mom and older sister were busy working on me, trying to get me ready because we were running out of time. My heart kept beating faster and faster, and I became more nervous as the moments passed. Mom put her hands on my face and looked into my eyes, as she always did, and assured me that everything would be all right. I wonder what she really felt in her heart, and how did she hide it so well?

As my thoughts ran wild, someone knocked on the door. "Time's up. They're starting. Are you ready in there?" The words echoed through my mind.

"Am I ready?" I thought, as we opened the door and waited for the cue for me to go to the top of the steps.

I could hear the music start as I approached the top of the staircase. My long train was behind me, as well as my little sister Judy who would carry my train down the steps. My oldest sister was in front of me dressed in her white and red maid of honor's gown. Mom put the Bible in my hand and the flowers on top of the Bible, gently kissed me, and went down the steps. The time had arrived.

As the bridal march started, my sister went down first, then I followed, taking each step with fear as well as excitement until I noticed I had reached the bottom and could see the people waiting for my arrival. Then as I reached the bottom of the steps, where my dad placed his arm into mine to continue with the march, my eyes were quickly drawn past the doors that divided me from the guests and straight to where HE was standing. There stood my Prince Charming, my knight in shining armor, standing by the preacher with tears coming out of his eyes. I felt so much happiness; I just knew this feeling would never end.

My dad and I continued through the huge foyer and into the living room until we stood in front of the pastor. The pastor then started the ceremony by asking, "Who gives this bride away?"

My dad quickly answered, "I and her mother," then slowly stepped away, and I stood side by side with my groom.

The pastor told us to turn toward each other and for John to take hold of my right hand as he proclaimed our marriage vows, and I hung onto every word uttered. The pastor then looked at me and said, "Debra, will you have this man to be your husband, to live together in the covenant of marriage? Will you love him, comfort him, honor and keep him, in sickness and in health, and forsaking all others, be faithful to him as long as you both shall live?"

With trembling in my voice, I said, "I do."

Then he turned to John and asked him the same questions. He stood there, tears running down his eyes as he looked into mine and slowly said, "I do."

Then the pastor continued, "Be fruitful and multiply, and now by the power invested in me, by God and the state of Kentucky, I pronounce you man and wife." Then he prayed that that we'd always put God first and always seek council with the Lord. It seemed that at that time, we both agreed till time moved forward.

He then looked at us both and said, "You may kiss your bride." We kissed for the first time in front of people, which was very hard for me, especially since Mom was watching, but I got through it.

At last, the pastor introduced us to our guests as Mr. and Mrs. Henry and invited everyone to stay and celebrate with us. We made our way to the dining room where the beautiful cake lay in wait for us to make our memories, and presents covered the top of the hutch as well as a crystal candelabra with red candles attached.

We did all the things that normally take place at a reception. We laughed; we cried and talked with each guest, then cut the cake and fed a bite to each other as my brother told John to shove it all over my face. But looking at me pleading, "No, it will mess up my hair and makeup," he gently put it in my mouth. It seemed everyone, for once, was happy as they normally are at weddings, and the time came for us to exit the party.

We had borrowed my mom's car because we didn't have one, but John promised he would get us one. My brothers, sister, friends, and family had decorated the car while the reception was going on. Now we were ready for the honeymoon. Finally, we would be on our way.

Everybody kissed us goodbye and bid us a good time. Mom, of course, with sadness in her eyes, told us to be careful and told John he'd better watch over me, which he assured her he would. As we drove off, my brother and cousin tried to keep up with us, but John lost them after a few minutes.

I had dreamed of what a honeymoon would be like, but guess what, it didn't happen like that. John quickly let me know that he didn't eat in any kind of restaurants, so I would go inside a fast-food restaurant, and we would go back to our hotel room. My fantasy dream was to go to a nice restaurant, order, and be waited on while we were dressed up, you know, like you see people going on dates in the movies. But this wasn't the movies, and I quickly got the picture that this type of behavior wouldn't change, and it didn't.

Back at the hotel, I can tell you I did not know what to expect, for Mom had not prepared me for what was coming that night, but I will just say that I wish she had. Maybe I would not have been that scared. I will go as far as to say I stayed in the bathroom for hours, scared to come out in my robe and gown, but eventually had to give way to marriage, and the night moved in with me becoming his wife and maintaining wifely duties.

We went on our honeymoon for three days, which was filled with excitement, probably some of the happiest moments that there would be for the next fifteen years. Then the honeymoon was over, and we were on our way back home.

CHAPTER 3

Who Is This Man (Jekyll or Hyde)?

When we returned, the family had our room ready, with fresh linens and all the accommodations a hotel would carry. Our pillows even had a fresh chocolate mint on them. I had such a caring family that believed even this marriage, with the help of Jesus, just might work, despite their many doubts in the past.

Things went well the first two weeks, which was some of the happiest moments of my life. I just knew everyone saw how wrong they had all been and we were going to make it and would be happy.

Just as I thought we'd live happily ever after, a change came that changed my life. It was a Friday night like no other night, one I would remember to write about.

On Friday nights in the Jackson house, you wouldn't find anyone at home because everyone would go out to eat at McDonald's, then visit Kmart for the blue light specials. Then it was on to the grocery store to buy the week's groceries. It was a family event, and everyone went.

We were given our weekly allowance and used it wisely. I think I had become the blue light special queen. If you wanted to find a bargain, just contact me. Of course, I didn't go because I was married, and my husband had not returned from work. I assumed he was working overtime, which meant more money for us to start our lives with.

I had dreams of moving out, but first we needed to save for a car. He was still driving my mom's car. The family would stay out till eleven or twelve o'clock, which was after all the stores closed.

On this night, I was the only one home, as everyone else had left to eat, but I was waiting for my husband. Seven o'clock passed, then seven-thirty. I was taking down the curlers in my hair when John's car pulled up at approximately seven forty-five. With excitement, I ran to the front door to greet him.

When John entered the room, I knew something was wrong, but I didn't know what. As I tried to kiss him, he pushed me away and said we were going to his mother's house. His mother lived seventy-five miles away, and I had never met her in the three years I'd known him. Whenever he talked about her, it was to call her a name or condemn her for something she had done in the past. I had tried to convince him to invite her to the wedding, but he had refused repeatedly. You can understand how this came as a shock.

My immediate words were, "I'm not dressed yet," meaning that if I were going to meet his family, I wanted some time to fix up just a little, for this would be an exciting and special moment for me. I wanted him to be proud of me, and besides, first impressions were important.

But he didn't wait for any explanation. The minute I started to get dressed, his countenance changed and went into a rage something I had only seen on television or at the movies. But this was real. He began to accuse me of not wanting to meet his mother and that I thought I was better than her because I was a Christian.

From that point, things progressed very quickly, but I remember every detail as if it was yesterday. I remember him saying to get in the car in a tone of voice in which I knew not to speak or move unless he told me to. I got in the car, and how we made it to the freeway, I'll never know. His eyes were like glass, and he was as cold as the icebergs of Alaska.

I thought to myself, "Am I in a nightmare?" He screamed at the top of his lungs as I sat next to him as we drove, saying everything he could think of as well as calling me every name in the book. I had never been treated this way or heard the kind of words that came from his mouth. I tried to hold back the tears, but they kept coming, but tears were not what he wanted to see.

After we drove approximately thirty miles up the freeway, he pulled into a rest area. For the first time in our marriage, he became physically violent. He told me he was not about to take me to his mother's after the way I had acted and that he would leave me there at the rest area, and I could get home the best way I knew how. Suddenly, he reached and grabbed a big chunk of my hair, dragged me out of the car and down the sidewalk, and threw me down to the ground. There were so many people who could see us, but none came to my rescue.

Next, he staggered back to the car and sped away, the wheels hitting the curb as he went out the exit. I stood there, trying to compose myself and not cry. I made my way to the restroom to try and fix my hair and compose myself.

Here I was, barely eighteen and already pregnant, stranded in a rest area, in a state of shock and terrified, not knowing what to do. What had I done, what had gone wrong, and what was wrong with him?

As I went to find a phone, not knowing whom to call because I knew there was no one at home, two men approached me. They had been watching as everything had happened. They asked if I was alright and if they could help. I replied no because I was so embarrassed, not knowing what to say and wanting to hide my face.

Suddenly, I heard a loud screeching sound, looked to see what it was, and saw John's car going backward, headed toward me. My heart started pounding, for I didn't know whether to run and hide or wait for him because I needed to get back home. It was too late to decide; he was suddenly there in front of me, telling me to get in the car, "I'm taking you home."

I got in the car, not knowing what to expect and kept very quiet as we drove off; as to where, I wasn't sure. We continued going north as though we were going toward where his family lived.

Just as quickly, John took an exit, then screamed that he wasn't going to see that old "B" and got back on the freeway going south. Still in a car of silence, the road finally looked like we were headed back to our house. I dared to ask but still prayed that was where we were headed.

Can you imagine how I felt? I had never been around somebody like this. My mind raced with thoughts of how I would explain this to my family. While the thoughts rushed through my head, we pulled up in front of the house.

In my heart, I hoped that someone would be home, but there were no cars visible, and upon going through the front door, I quickly saw no one was home. I was alone to defend for myself. A million thoughts went through my mind; what would happen next? I didn't know this person, and I didn't trust him anymore. All the thoughts were of fear, anger, and hurt.

As we walked inside, I entered first, with the door shutting behind him as he entered. At that sound, I begged God to not let me get hurt. Now I wonder why I didn't try to run, but I was too frightened. All I can tell you is that I didn't walk very far, for I was waiting and trembling to receive my next order.

John looked at me with devilish eyes and explained, "If you ever do this to me again, this is what is going to happen to you."

In horror, I watched as he turned into a raving lunatic. He began turning over furniture, destroying anything that could be destroyed. He even turned over a large birdcage with a parrot in it that took off flying. I stood paralyzed, not knowing what to do. Should I run or stand there? But my body had just shut down, and I was frozen. It seemed like it lasted an eternity, but I can't tell you how long it took for him to destroy the downstairs of our house.

As I slowly looked around, I could see even the pictures hanging on the walls had been turned upside down.

Suddenly, John turned and looked at me with eyes full of hate as he turned toward the front door and walked over to it and walked quickly out.

As I heard the car screech off, for the first time that evening, I felt safe, at least for a while. I stood there with the tears beginning to flow, first quietly, then my weeping turned into a loud hysterical cry while slumping down slowly to the floor, my face covered by my hands.

After sitting on the floor for a few minutes, I composed myself, and my thoughts began to wander. "What am I going to say or do when my mom and family get home?"

Just then, I heard a car pull up. That feeling of sickness came into the pit of my stomach, and I didn't want to be here. I wanted to hide if it was John, so I peeked out the window and saw it was my part of my family.

At that moment, I just wanted everything to go away, everything to be perfect, just like my dream of him had been. I didn't want to face my family. Why couldn't it just go away? As I kept repeating everything in my head, the door opened.

As each family member came through the door, they appeared to be speechless, using a lot of hand gestures with their mouths hanging open.

Then Mom spoke up. "What happened?" as she bent down beside me, embracing me. I began to cry hysterically as my head lay on her shoulder, explaining between sobs and trying to compose myself as much as possible. I told her I really didn't know what had happened. (I believe I was in a state of shock.) I had no answers and couldn't speak, trying hard to hold back the tears. I remember I felt like Mom could take all the pain away, but coming back to reality this time, it wouldn't go away.

Each member had his or her own comments, which all included killing John, but after everything that had happened, I kept trying to find some kind of excuse on why he did it. But no excuse sounded good enough. The comments came one by one and went on for what seemed like forever.

Eventually, they stopped, and Mom came forward and told them we needed to stop and start cleaning up the mess. The next few hours were spent with every one cleaning up and fixing what could be fixed, and the rest went to the trash.

Just as we were finishing up and things were starting to calm down, the front doorbell rang. As I sat on the couch, Mom moved toward the door to answer it. As she opened it, I heard her say angrily, "What are you doing here?"

The voice on the other side responded with, "I left something here."

Mom replied, "What?"

He said, "My wife."

At that point, I watched Mama melt as she pulled John in the front door, explaining, as he cried, what he had done. He stated he was drunk and couldn't help himself. I waited under the stairwell, peeking out in the darkness and listening as she talked with him. I didn't want to see him or hear what he had to say, but at the same time, I knew Mama would take care of things.

Meanwhile, the rest of the family sat in the living room, listening and waiting like a pack of tigers to prance on him. He and Mom talked for what seemed like hours, and then I saw Mom pat him on the arm and pull him inside the door and say, "Go with your wife and talk with her in your bedroom. The Lord will help you change as time goes on."

In fear, I walked with him toward the room, closing the door behind us while thinking about how I wished Mom could go in there with us. But Mom went toward the living room to speak and calm down the rest of the family.

Mom was the leader of our house, and what she said went, so it didn't matter how angry anybody was, nobody stepped out of bounds with Mom, and she made sure of that. On the other hand, Mom had a heart of gold and forgiveness, along with believing that anyone could be changed by the power of Jesus.

That night, before he passed out, John apologized and said he would never hurt me again. The worse part about it was that I believed him. If I had only known then what I know now I would have walked away and not looked back.

While reading this book, if you are hurting or know you are in this same situation, please get help. And if you don't know Jesus, it is a good time to ask Him into your heart and contact someone.

CHAPTER 4

Watch Out for All the Curves

A month later we found out I was pregnant, which was a blessing from the Lord. The event was welcome throughout the household, even by John. This would be the first grandchild for my mom.

The news was very scary for me, considering my mom had not been very open to talk to me about sex before our marriage, let alone telling me how a baby came to be or the process that followed. It was a hushed subject in our household, so you learned as the game was played. It was like walking in a dark room being blind, and having no one there to help lead you. Being raised that way was very uncomfortable; having no one to talk to, not even John. I couldn't bring myself to even ask him, so quietness was kept very well.

About two months after the marriage, Mom lost the big house we had married in. She never mentioned us contributing rent or monies to help her out or to pay our way, and being young, I didn't even think about it, which was so out of the game. She thought she was helping us out, but it just gave John room to use his money for his pleasures and a small amount to what I needed, which was very little.

Dad was gone, so Mom had very little money to work with except child support. Most women back then stayed home and cooked, cleaned, did the laundry, and whatever they could find to do to make extra money. Mom was always working, and her lawyer told her that's why the divorce laws had created alimony and more child support than the minimum, but she couldn't bring herself to do that. She had never worked outside of the home except when she was fifteen but she wasn't married. In the church world back then, women did not work out if married, at least in the churches we attended.

Then Mom had us six children with no job experience. Raising us was her life. Mom was good about never discussing her financial problems. She was a warrior and always leaned completely on the Lord. She would say, "God will provide for us," and I can say, He always did.

One of the ways God provided (or I thought He provided) was Lee moved in with us to help with the rent as a boarder.

When we had to move out, Lee had a friend who was in construction and had an apartment that was vacant. He said we could stay there till we found a house. So we moved. This was a studio apartment, which consisted of a small kitchen big enough to squeeze a small table with two chairs in an alcove area, a bathroom, and a very large living room/bedroom.

Since John and I were married, and I was pregnant, they gave us the master bedroom, which we all joked and called it our suite, really being the alcove of the kitchen. The bed came a few feet from reaching the refrigerator, settling tightly in a little alcove area where a table would have been. At night, the kitchen was closed, so everybody knew to stay away to give us some privacy.

Our family consisted of eight more members: my mom, Lee, three sisters, two brothers, and John's youngest brother, who had come to live with us because he had been kicked out by his mom and had no place to go. He was five years younger than John and was a twin to another brother.

I bet you're wondering where everyone else slept? The living room was the chosen place. On the floor at night, all the rest of the family would sleep on sleeping bags, and by morning, they'd all get rolled up and put away till the next night.

Mom had always wanted to start an orphanage for boys, and I guess this is how she fulfilled her dream by always taking in kids who had no place to go. She always thought she could save and rehabilitate them.

The next few years would prove that, for, in time, she would house all of John's brothers at different times, as well as one of his sisters, who married my oldest brother years later and is still married to him after thirty years of marriage at this writing.

All in all, we got along pretty well most of the time, even though we were all cooped up. Sometimes we would all start laughing at just anything, but it sure felt good inside.

As the next few months progressed on, things seemed to go great for a while. But then, like a road with many curves, the one I was on seemed to have no straight parts. Being pregnant at first seemed to make John very happy, and things went pretty smooth, but then came one of those curves, and it was very winding.

I was close to being six months along and was still trying to hang on to a gift God had given me, which was my singing. Our family trio had been invited to sing at a huge conference in West Virginia from Saturday to Sunday. The whole family had been invited as well, and we were supposed to leave Friday night, for it was an all-night drive. John had known about this trip and had agreed he would go all the way up to Friday night when we were supposed to leave.

On that day, he came home, and I had everything packed and ready to go, for it was a seven-hour trip, and we would get there in the early hours of Saturday morning. Right after he got home, he said his boss had told him they really needed him to work on Saturday and he couldn't go. He said he felt really bad and was sorry, but didn't want to lose his job, and he gently kissed me on the forehead.

Being six months pregnant with our next child, I really wanted him to go, but I didn't emotionally get into it, and it was time to go. I also needed to do this for me. This would be our first time apart since we had been married. I chose to believe him, but it would be the first of many tales on a very curvy road that went on for years and years.

I felt in my heart if John had gone to the conference, it would have helped him to grow in the Lord, or if he was lost, he could accept the Lord, but that didn't happen.

I always had the reality that church never hurt anybody, and I still stand upon those words today. And because I had lived a sheltered life with problems, I felt going to church made your life easier (which it does), but I thought no problems would come your way.

Was I wrong, and did I have a lot of growing up to do. At eighteen, I found out you didn't know it all and just the opposite. When following Jesus, the devil would hit you in full force, and your testimony was born.

We went and were blessed with three days of great worship and great preaching, which I needed. After we got back, I was bringing clothes in from the car, and a young girl who lived in an apartment downstairs stopped me and said she would like to talk with me and asked me to come into her apartment. I didn't know her, but I knew she acted like it was a very serious matter. After inviting me to sit down, she explained that what she was about to tell me was something that would hurt me, but she felt obligated to do so.

She said she had been watching and observing me since the day we had moved in and learned very quickly that I was a very innocent young lady who was very naive to the world around me. "And . . . I don't think life is very fair to you, for you don't deserve what your husband is doing to you."

By this time, besides feeling very sick to my stomach and embarrassed as well as shy, I couldn't imagine what she was talking about, but I wanted her to get to the point, even though I couldn't bring myself to say it.

This woman continued by saying, "While you were gone, your husband had a much older woman than himself staying in your apartment for the whole weekend." She said she had seen them kissing in the car before getting out to start upstairs. "Now honey, she didn't sleep on the floor, and she didn't leave till early Sunday night."

As she described the woman, tears flowed down my cheeks, yet I held back the sound, not only because I was hurt but because I was so ashamed in front of this stranger, having a hard time speaking to anyone I didn't know because of my shyness.

I was torn apart between being scared that my family would find out and my heart being totally broken and not knowing how to address the problem. Who could I talk to? There was no one. I didn't even try God.

That night I tried to address the problem very quietly in the kitchen (our bedroom), so no one could hear from the living room, but then John's anger appeared like magic; one moment, he was kind and loving, and the next, he was a person with glassy eyes who would have frightened the devil himself. Then the violence begin.

Within a few moments, he placed both his hands tightly around my neck and started choking me till I couldn't breathe. I fought back, trying to free myself, but his strength overpowered me until I passed out. Even then at that moment, when I was fighting him with all my strength for what seemed like an eternity, I was still trying to protect him and hold back the scream so my family couldn't hear me.

I couldn't understand why God didn't step in and stop him, but I knew it was He who intervened at the right moment so that I didn't lose my life and survived.

Many of you are thinking, "What kind of loving God wouldn't stop the incident from happening altogether? But you are forgetting our free will. God is a gentleman and allows us the right to make our own choices that design our lives. But it is up to us to ask for His direction about everything.

We either allow Him to direct our paths, or we take the path that we choose to create, which is not straight but curvy and with many turns. More than less, in our younger years as adults, we make our own path and, in time, decide after many failures to allow him the open door to cultivate us and mold us into His image, but not until after much heartache.

Now I look back to that moment when I was scared to scream, and I can decipher it. What was the answer? I felt scared, but at the same time I wanted to protect him or protect our marriage and didn't want the family to think we were failing. I couldn't face that I hadn't married a knight in shining armor. And as time progressed, I would recognize nothing was ever perfect except Christ, and I wasn't close.

We had our first child nine months and seven days after our marriage. We had a beautiful baby girl. It was just what John and I had wanted. To me, there could not have been any greater joy. But with all the new bundle of joy, I couldn't help but think lying in the hospital bed, even as I had carried our child, John had chosen to be unfaithful, and if that wasn't enough, he took off while I was in the hospital to continue his unfaithfulness and drinking. I chose to stay silent and say nothing but pondered so much in my heart.

The lies and abuse continued throughout the years. Time after time, he talked his way out of the lies and back into my heart, proving to me he was innocent and I was guilty of not being the wife I should be. Every time he cheated, left, or abused me, the situation seemed to get turned around. I didn't show him enough attention, take care of him, or so on . . . da, da, da, and to the contrary, I continued to believe in him.

After a few months had gone by, we turned another sharp curve. One Saturday morning, one of my cousins called and asked if John would help him move. He said he'd only need him for a few hours. He stated he needed his muscles for heavy lifting, which John had.

At around 8 a.m. John kissed me and the baby goodbye and said he'd be back soon. But 8 a.m. turned into noon, and then ten o'clock that night came around, and still no John. By now, I had learned that if he was late, something was up.

Mom always knew but tried not to make it obvious. Out of the blue, she would say she needed to go get something from the store. It was like we could all read her mind. We all knew she was going to spy on John to see if he was up to one of his tricks and lies. She was trying to spare me, but we all decided we wanted to go to the store. So all of us crammed into the car and, sure enough, that's where she was going.

As we pulled up in front of the duplex, we noticed two silhouettes behind the window shade embracing in the duplex next door to my cousin's. The man's silhouette looked just like John.

As I got out of the car, the lights suddenly went off, and I tried to ignore the rush of fear coming over me. As I pulled myself together, fighting back the tears and trying to deny what my eyes had just seen, I walked up to the screened front door, where I could see my cousin and his wife sitting and watching TV.

I knocked, said hi, and then asked where John was. At this point, both began to look very nervous and tried to stall me with an answer, not knowing what to say. But suddenly out of breath, John appeared in sight and said, "Here I am, I've been in the bathroom."

I did not know the rest of my family was out in the car witnessing the rest of the story. As I was going to my cousin's door, they heard a door slam, then saw a woman run from behind the duplex next door and toward the back of my cousin's duplex. Seconds later, they saw John run from the same duplex to the back of my cousin's duplex and heard another door slam.

By this time, Mom had made her way to where I was. She barged in and started yelling, "Debbie he was in the house next door with another woman. She's either in here or the adjoining duplex."

At that moment, we heard a door slam from the back of the duplex again and the back door to the other duplex open and slam shut. I knew she was in there but didn't know what to do. My cousin said he wasn't involved, and we needed to leave and take John with us. He said he didn't need the problems; he had enough of his own.

Believe it or not, we left with John, but neither of us spoke, and in the car, the atmosphere was the same. It was a quiet ride home, and I wondered why nobody was jumping his case, but I guess they were waiting on Momma to say something, and that was that. I look back now and wonder why I even stayed at this point; we had been married only two years, and so much had gone on. Not only were these situations happening often, but the physical abuse was also getting worse and harder to hide.

Soon we moved from the small apartment to a huge, beautiful house in a small town (Nicholasville) in Kentucky, not far away. The house was a two-story that had been built in the early 1900s for the rich who had servants. There were two sets of steps, the main winding stairwell in the front of the house and a very narrow and steep set of steps in the back of the house that ended at the kitchen.

At the top of the main stairs stood a long corridor that extended past four doors on each side and ended up facing a small room that had once been the servant's quarters. Right outside the servant's quarter's door stood the top of the small stairwell that landed at the back entrance of the kitchen.

Each of the doors along the corridor opened up into a humongous suite-style bedroom. These rooms measured approximately thirty by thirty and were twenty feet high. One of those rooms belonged to John and me. Of course, moving from a small studio apartment with very little privacy to a house that looked like it came out of the movie *Gone with the Wind* made our relationship stand more solid for a while. But no matter where we were, it seemed John grew restless and wanted freedom. And, of course, it showed.

We quickly became friends with one of my favorite cousins, Darlene and her husband, Tommy which was an awesome thing, for we never went out with friends and socialized, but John always found time to go out by himself.

We started getting very close to them and did everything together. It was good to have friends our age who didn't live with us. They didn't live too far from us, which allowed us to spend a great deal of time together.

John was in drywall, which paid good money. He even got my cousin's husband a job, which allowed them to ride together. That left my cousin and me with a car to get around in as well. You see, I didn't know how to drive, and everybody said all the time that I didn't need to because it wasn't safe while being pregnant. Of course, that meant my cousin had to drive. And I accepted it because I was always pregnant! Oh yes, our second child was on the way.

It sure was a lot more fun to go with my cousin than with John. He complained any time he had to take me anywhere. He was very impatient and timed my visits. Most of the time, he pawned me off on my family, even for doctor visits.

After a few months, the bliss ended. My cousin confided in me that she and her husband were not getting along and something had changed him since he had started hanging around John. She said they argued continually, and she felt something was going on, but she didn't know what. She said that Tommy, her husband, was not good at lying or hiding anything and lately had been doing both. As usual, I tried to tell her and convince myself nothing was wrong, but I didn't make her feel any better.

Then the day came. It was an early Friday evening, and we were at my house waiting for John and Tommy to come home with their paychecks. Darlene was the type of woman who knew every penny her husband made and dictated where it would go. I, on the other hand, after being married a little over a year, knew better than to ask what John made and managed on what he always gave me.

Being very close, she informed me that John made a lot and should be giving me more to take care of us. She said I should find out what he was doing with his money. Although we were close, I couldn't share my thoughts with her or anyone and kept everything inside, but I was glad to have her by my side this day.

Six thirty rolled around, and she got tired of waiting and decided to call his work. The lady on the other end informed her that they had left a couple of hours before. As her call ended, she told me in a not-so-nice tone to get in the car, for we were going on a hunt.

We hadn't driven very far when we saw them pass us, but they were not going in the direction of our homes. They saw us as well and raced to get away from us. John was in the driver's seat and was laughing as we tried to catch up to them. At times, we went over the same streets till he eventually lost us.

I can tell you that I felt the same as I did when John tore up my house. I really felt sick and couldn't talk. Darlene was busy doing the talking for both of us as she frantically drove. What she had to say about John wasn't pleasant, and I won't write on paper, but most of it was the truth.

I had loved being close to her, but at this moment, I wish I hadn't been because anybody John became involved with became corrupted. Tommy had made his own decision, but John influenced everybody he was around. I always assumed he would pick up the good traits of people he was around, but that never seemed to happen.

Slowly, the anger turned into crying as we headed back toward my house, which I feared again, for I also had to face my family and later hers. Upon arriving and her telling the story, all the reaction was the same. No good words could be found for John. Anger went throughout the house again.

We had to figure out not only where they were but what were we going to use for money. We both lived paycheck to paycheck, but I at least lived with Mom. Darlene lived in a house where bills had to be paid, and now where was Tommy spending the money? Neither of us knew what lay ahead.

Darlene and I sat in a daze of disbelief of what had just unfolded in front of us and the uncertainty of not knowing what lay ahead for us when John's boss's wife suddenly called. Then things really fell apart.

She explained that after we called her, John had come back to her house and told her that a lady would be picking up money he owed her and if he could leave it with her. He continued to tell her that they were going to Florida for an emergency, and neither he nor Tommy would be coming back to work. She then asked him if it would be his wife, and he said no and described what the lady would look like.

After he left, his boss's wife got suspicious and decided to call his home number. Being an older, more mature woman, she sorted through things and said she knew John had kids and knew they needed his money. She continued and said that when the lady came to the door, she looked like a hooker, and she decided to tell her that John had left no money.

That's when John's boss's wife decided to call me. She asked if he had left me and if he had given me any money in doing so. I explained to her what happened and couldn't tell her if he had left, only that he hadn't come home and hadn't called. She gave me directions and told me to come and pick up the money, which we did.

Darlene ran me out there, but no words were exchanged, and the silence was as thick as an early morning autumn fog. We went to the door, chatted with his boss's wife, then she gave me an envelope with the money in it, hugged us both, and we went on our way. On our way back to my house, I told Darlene how sorry I was, but she just nodded, and the silence began again.

Upon dropping me off at my house, Darlene got out of the car, and we exchanged hugs, then she said she would call me tomorrow unless she heard of any news that night, then she drove off.

Two weeks passed, and we still had not heard anything from John or Tommy. My family had been gracious and took care of me, providing the necessities I needed for me and our daughter. This was the first time John had been gone over a few days. He would normally leave on a Friday when he got paid and come back after he had wasted all the money. Then he would come back and somehow make me feel like the guilty one, and I would carry him food to the room. I guess he didn't want to face the family.

A few months later, I received a call from Darlene saying Tommy had called her and begged her to let him come home. She said they were in Florida, living on the beach, him, John, and the girl who was supposed to get the money. She said the money was for her transportation to get down there. He also told her the girl was the same one he had been with in the apartment and at my cousin's house.

I remember Tommy came home that weekend and swore to her on his life that he would never get mixed up with someone like John again, and he'd never leave her, and to this day, I don't think he ever did. But our relationship as best friends ended. I was saddened, but this was who I had married, and once again, I was secluded from the world.

I am sorry to say at this writing my cousin Darlene, along with her husband, Tommy, has passed away. I did get one more chance to see her at my own mother's funeral in 1993. We embraced each other, but that was the last time I saw her.

By now, I was barely seven months pregnant and not feeling too good. It hurt that John had left me, but my family had made sure that I knew I was loved. I had to work around the days that they wanted to talk about him (which was almost every time they had to take me somewhere or fork out money, especially when I went to the doctor) because it always ended up that I was stupid, and in truth, I knew they were right, but they did nothing to help me figure a way out.

One Friday afternoon, I was with my mom and sisters. We had stopped to get something from a chicken place when upon coming out, I slid down the ramp. I landed flat on my butt. But I saved the bucket of chicken I was holding and managed to pick myself up. The manager ran out of the store to make sure I was alright, and I thought I was and assured him I was. I blamed the slippery sandals I had on and went on my way.

The following week I noticed some bleeding and told Mom about it. She immediately took me to the hospital to make sure everything was alright.

After telling them what had happened the previous week upon my examination, I was hospitalized.

I guess Mom somehow contacted John's mom, who, in return, had a way to contact John. When I had been in labor almost a week, the final hours came around. By now, I had wished everything had not happened and that John was here. Why did life have to be this way, and couldn't God just bring him back and change him?

Within three hours of them reeling me in to have the baby, John walked in, grabbing my hand and asking forgiveness for not being there and saying he'd always be by my side if I'd have him. And, of course, in my condition, I said yes and threw my arms around him. Within a few hours, we had a baby boy.

He had been born two months early and did have a few complications but had gotten through them, and we took him home.

After four days, we knew something was wrong because his eyes were completely yellow, and he couldn't eat. We went back to the hospital, where, upon examining him, they admitted him, telling us they thought he had spinal meningitis. John, of course, said it was God's way of punishing him because of what he had done, but Mom assured me everything would be alright; just stay in prayer. The doctors came in and told us they were going to do a spinal tap so they could accurately diagnose him and what steps was needed to treat him.

At this point, I had never met John's mother, only what she was like from John telling me how sad his past was. But on this occasion, he chose to go to the pay phone and call her. While crying and explaining to her that our baby might die, I suddenly heard him call her a foul name and angrily hang up the phone.

He rushed back to where we were sitting to repeat what she had told him. In shock, he said she told him if he died, we could always have another one. At his statement, I began to understand why John was the way he was. He needed counseling, but that didn't happen.

Our baby had been born at five pounds and thirteen ounces. Now he was down to four pounds, six ounces. They had diagnosed him with yellow jaundice, along with him having a breathing problem that caused him to stop breathing every few minutes. But they attached a little machine to his foot, and the machine would tap his foot to start his breathing again. He also couldn't eat, and they were going to start feeding him intravenous, but before they did that, Mom stepped in and said to try to feed him out of a little medicine bottle. I did, and it worked. So every day when I came to the hospital, I would stay all day, and he would drink out of his medicine bottle while my mom and sisters stayed home with my daughter.

We went back and forth to the hospital for the next four days, living by faith, and the whole family remained on their knees till the day came when all symptoms were gone, and we got to take our five-pound baby boy home. I thought everything would be okay and this would be my last child. Was I wrong on both?

CHAPTER 5

Let's Go All the Way to the Top

John and I seemed to grow closer over the next few months. John was working hard, and we were actually getting along. We had moved back out to Arizona, but after only a few months, my mom grew restless. She called a family meeting and asked if anybody would like to move to the mountains of Kentucky, and John was the first to raise his hands.

You have to understand that even though we were from Kentucky, we had never lived outside the city limits of Lexington and had moved to California, where we were raised. When we left Kentucky, my sibling's ages ranged from four to fourteen, me being ten. The only time we ever spent in small towns was when my dad preached in the Kentucky Mountains. I guess you can say we really faced country life, and what an experience.

John was an outdoorsman and was all for the move, and I thought the change would do us good. How Mom ever picked Stanton, I don't remember, but the next thing I knew, it was fall, and we had to find a house. Stanton was a small town in the middle of the state with a population of about four thousand at that time.

And if you're wondering if I am pregnant again, yep; baby number three was on the way.

I can assure you after we were there just a few days, everyone knew who we were, and we were the talk of the town. Not many strangers came through and certainly not from out west. Here we were, four young girls (one being me), along with three young men (one being John), then there was my mom and soon-to-be stepdad.

I was the only one married and was pregnant, but you couldn't tell. I can tell you this, within one day, everybody of this small town knew our names and where we were from, and everywhere we went, we gathered stares.

For you to understand the atmosphere change we made, you must first know a few facts. In the mountains of Kentucky back then (now things have changed), people married their distant cousins a lot because almost everybody was related in some way or another. You've probably heard one of the redneck jokes about when you're hunting a wife or husband in this neck of the woods; you go to a family reunion. It really wasn't a joke; they had to marry someone related to them because not many outsiders lived there.

We were breaking their cycle. Not only were we exciting because we weren't related to them, but we were also from California.

And I can tell you this; it didn't take much time for my sisters to notice there were a lot of good-looking mountain men. And the guys of the town, they stared like they had never seen girls before. Hunting season was definitely in the air.

As we drove many curvy country roads over the next few weeks, we knew winter was not far off, and we needed to find a house. We drove up a road, and only because it was autumn could we see through the massive amount of trees a house that looked like it was not lived in.

After driving back the rocky, curvy mile-long driveway, we finally reached an empty house that could be turned into our home. It was a fix-er-upper but would be beautiful when we got done with it.

We stopped at the little country store close to the property and found out who owned it, and they gave us the information we needed, and next thing we knew, we had leased our new home.

After a week of hard work, we had a beautiful four-bedroom with a bathroom. (We girls all loved it because over half the houses back then didn't have bathrooms inside, so we were shouting, "Hallelujah! Thank you, Jesus.")

We soon found out that it had one of the highest peaks privately owned in the state of Kentucky. The name was State Rock, and it was well known by many who came from miles away to climb it. It was noted for being a romance spot for couples to view the gorgeous countryside, and after moving in, we were no exception to the rule.

The house sat in the midst of 125 acres of pure beauty. There was a forest of cherry, walnut, oak, and knotty pine trees, along with many fruit trees, some of the best apple, pear, peach, and cherry trees you could find. Oh, and don't let me forget about the best blackberries, strawberries, and mushrooms you could ever put into your mouth.

Then there were every kind of flowers that bloomed from hill to hill, along with many different types of birds and wild animals, which included bears and mountain lions.

We even had two good-sized lakes that housed fish for the taking, along with natural springs with crystal clear water flowing from their mouths. The rest of the farm bore some of the most beautiful hillsides covered with moss and hidden caves. For nature lovers, this was the ideal oasis on earth to live and raise a family.

Before long, we had settled in and made this our hometown. The best news I had was that John was in love with it.

I must stop for a moment to comment on just how hard it was for all of my family to grow accustomed to the mountain way of life. I have chosen one story to share with you and will take a quick break from the source of the story to share a little bit of humor, and then we will move on.

When we moved into this beautiful piece of property, we were told by the landlord we would have to keep up with the allotment of tobacco crop that was included in the land we leased and it would financially pay us for the work. None of my family smoked except Lee and John. But we weren't strangers to it, for we had an uncle who had raised tobacco as far back as I could remember and had been very successful with it. We had visited him throughout the years before moving out west and had played in the barns and fields as they harvested the tobacco. Many times Mom would go cook and help my aunt prepare the meals to feed the workers.

To make a long story short, all the adults who lived in our house decided, "How hard could it be?" I was the only one excused from working the fields because, of course, I was pregnant, and this one time, I was so happy. I had watched from my uncle's house so many times and knew how dirty of a job it was between the smell and the sticky substance that got all over your hands when housing time came around in the fall.

The men in the family, not having much knowledge, went and purchased the tobacco plants by a card that was on record of how much their allotment was. It was my stepdad, John, my brother, and two mountain guys, who later became two of my brothers-in-law. They, along with my mom and sisters, planted, cultivated, and in the fall, housed it in the barn. I can tell you, they all worked very hard.

It takes from early spring to late fall to grow and harvest tobacco. Then the time comes to take it to the market to sell. That's what this part of my story is about. If you remember, we had never lived in the country and didn't smoke or knew very little about raising a crop, just what my family researched, and there was no internet at the time, so that meant talking to mountain folks.

The big day finally came when the tobacco was ready to be taken to the market. We were assured by my two soon-to-be brothers-in-law that the quality of the tobacco was very good, but they forgot to tell us about quantity.

The guys decided to go in our old Cadillac, and they loaded the tobacco into the big trunk. By now, if you know anything about raising tobacco, you're probably already on the floor laughing. But for all you who don't, let me continue my story.

The guys had smiles on their faces when they left our farm and headed to the market. Now the market means the place where you sell tobacco, not the store market. Upon their arrival, they were instructed to pull through the line so that the tobacco could be inspected to see the quality of the plants.

They continued driving through the inspection line until it was their turn, then all five exited the vehicle. The inspector inspected and previewed all the tobacco and said it was very good quality, and they would get a great price for it. But as he turned and looked at each one of them, he asked, "Will the trucks be following soon, and how many trucks are there?"

What the guys didn't know was the allotment for our land was an enormous amount of tobacco, and they had only brought in one car trunk load.

They stared at each other and waited for each other to speak up, each of them wanting to find the nearest hole to crawl into.

Lee stepped up and said, "Sir, this is the whole crop," and by now, there was quite a few more men standing around, and each held back their snickers and expressions, for they all knew who we were, and after that, we were the laughingstock of the town. You can figure out the rest of the story.

After the tobacco tale and other wild stories, we got accustomed to our new lives. Two of my sisters started dating two of the mountain boys, who turned out to be distant cousins, and they helped us to adjust as much as we could. Both sisters in a short time married those two mountain boys.

As time passed, in our front yard under a beautiful trellis that was covered with roses, my brother married his fiancée, and six months later, one of my sisters married a mountain man.

John, as usual, did his own thing and would go out and stay gone all night and sometimes for weeks, but we managed to stay together. The arguments continued, and somehow he always convinced me he wasn't with anybody, just hunting, fishing, or hanging out with the boys. Yet there were plenty of tales and eyewitnesses, but I chose to close my eyes and look the other way to have some peace and a little bit of happiness. You might not understand what I mean by this statement unless you have been in a situation of like manner, but hopefully through this testimony, you'll understand what it's like and how the mind works when you're abused.

I found out later that the word went around very quickly that I was known as John's woman; you didn't look at or touch, and if you did you'd face the fist of Big Bad John.

As the months passed, I my belly grew bigger, and I needed to be with family, but John was hardly around. No matter what I tried, nothing seemed to ever stop John's wild streak. At the same time, his jealousy was more than I could bear. I walked on eggshells when he was around because I didn't want to make him mad or get slapped. What I didn't know then was that when someone was that jealous, it was usually because they were guilty of what they were accusing you.

Boys came over all the time to see my sisters, but I couldn't make myself invisible. All the young people would get together and just sit and talk for hours. I tried to stay in our bedroom, but I was so lonely and wanted to have friends my age. I was only nineteen with two little ones and one in the oven. I would come out of the room when they fell asleep. I was so scared to get too much into the conversation, for I knew John could come home at any moment, so I kept my visits to a minimum.

I found myself diving deeper into John's control and moved into a shell that protected me as well as kept me alive.

CHAPTER 6

A Week in a Country Jail

One Friday night, while going through tobacco season, three or four young men came over to hang out with my family just to have some honest clean fun. We spent most of the night sitting around the table while talking and playing many different games, earning some well-deserved relaxation. The whole group had worked very hard between raising the crop and tending the garden. And like a normal weekend, John had gone out, which included no family, only his friends and the games they played, including drinking, getting high, and loose women.

One of the young men (my soon-to-be brother-in-law) invited a good friend of his over, and he brought a couple of six packs of soda for all of us to share while we provided the chips, dip, cookies, and games.

I always felt more at ease when John was gone because I didn't have to be on guard and could act like the young person I was. I decided to join in and play some games with them instead of just watching kids, cooking, or cleaning. I was already the mother of two and pregnant again and still just nineteen. John had been gone a few days, so I decided to take a leap of faith. I needed friends my own age to have fun with, and this night was a night like that. How I would come to regret that decision.

Somehow that same night, word got back to John that I was there with one of the young men who had brought the soda and that he had come to see me, which was so far from the truth. I don't even think I spoke to him except when we played Monopoly. But John did find out and this is what was relayed to me by the police.

As the end of the night unfolded, John being high on drugs as well as being fully intoxicated, parked and waited for the young man at an old target range, which was located at the bottom of the hill where locals like John frequently hung out. He stood by a rock close to the road and waited in the dark till he saw the young man approaching. There was only one way up the mountain and one way down, so John knew he had to come his way.

As the young man got closer, John walked out into the road and flagged him down. He told the young man that he had been target practicing, his car wouldn't start, and he need a jump. So the young man pulled off the road.

Immediately upon approaching the truck, John started accusing him of being with me. The young man tried to convince him otherwise, but John, in his state of mind, didn't listen. He jerked the door open and quickly pulled the young man from his truck and threw him to the ground and started punching him profusely. At that point, he didn't care who was watching and assumed no one could stop him. Thank God, someone in a nearby house was watching and saw what was happening and immediately called the police, and they rushed within minutes to the scene.

When they arrived, the boy was lying on the ground, not moving much, and John was hovering over him, continuing the beating. Two policemen encountered a severe scuffle with John trying to subdue him, but together they couldn't contain him. They had called for more help, and two became eight. As the fight rolled on, it took the eight policemen to restrain him enough to place handcuffs on him and arrest him. The final blow was with a Billie club, which landed him in the hospital to be stitched up, then on to jail he went. When I called to check on him, the dispatcher told me he had been knocked unconscious and needed quite a few stitches. I can't believe I actually cried, wondering how bad he was hurt. They said he was fine and told me I could come down and see him the next morning if I wanted to.

As well they reported to me the young man was in bad shape, and John had almost succeeded in killing him.

I felt like a bad person and somehow convinced myself it was all my fault and I should have just stayed in my room that night. I felt so bad for the young man. I reasoned in my mind all the maybes of what I should have done or should not have done. If only I had stayed in my room, none of this would have happened. But now, I must work on fixing the issue at hand. I knew I wouldn't be able to sleep, and that was the truth. All night long, I cried out to God and asked Him what I should do, and then I asked Him to help me get John out, and, "oh God, fix him."

Before I move on I must speak to the one who is reading this book, and I ask you again, are you in a similar situation right now? God doesn't want you to be abused. God doesn't make any junk. Tell someone and GET HELP!

I found out later that night through my sister's boyfriend that his sister was the clerk of the jail, and his brother-in-law was the sheriff. The jail was in their house like so many other jails in small country towns, but I was in for a shock the next morning.

The next morning when I entered the front door of their house, I thought I had entered into Mayberry, USA. I quickly gazed past the entryway that ended at the start of the jail. To my left was the kitchen, and behind that the hallway that led to the rest of the house. The jail consisted of two cells that sat side by side. One was locked, which was the one John was in. The other they didn't, which was for the locals. After looking around, I decided I had come to Mayberry and wondered where Barney and Andy were. As I looked into the cells, there were only two inmates, one of which was John, and the other looked like Otis (the weekend drunk) from the *Andy Griffith Show*.

As I inspected the cell that John was in, the other cellmate yelled over to the woman in the kitchen to ask what they were having for breakfast, and she yelled back that they were having biscuits and gravy. The next thing I knew, the prisoner opened the door of his cell and went to the kitchen to fix him some biscuits and gravy.

The only prisoner left in the cells was John, so I walked over and stood at the window to talk to him about what had happened. As I stared at him, I shook my head with disapproval of what he had done as my eyes went straight to the stitches that had been sewn into his swollen forehead above his eyebrow. We exchanged words, but mine seemed to get drowned out by his words, "How are you going to get me out of this place?"

I waited for an apology, but as usual, it didn't come. His words led quickly to it being my job to get him out, no matter the cost. He said we'd discuss everything else after he got out but also included how much he missed me as he pushed his arms out through the bars and pulled my face close to his so he could kiss me.

It's like he had gone to drama school and knew exactly what to say and how to act to get me to do just as he wanted. I was like a puppet, and he pulled the strings. Puppets don't speak, and they do only what the puppeteer wants them to do.

Throughout the next week, I spent each day visiting him as well as running errands he told me to do so that he could get out of jail. But this meant someone in the family had to take me; I couldn't drive and had to be chauffeured around. Till the writing of these stories, I never realized how much time I required of them and how much they sacrificed for me. They may have fussed with me, but in the end, they always showed me mercy.

When the day arrived for court, John's bail was set at five thousand dollars, which I had to beg Mom to pay, but she did, and he was released.

As usual, upon his arrival home, he apologized for what he had done but explained to me he was so jealous and loved me so much and didn't like it when I was around other guys. I tried to explain to him that nothing had happened, but my words went out the window, as they always did when it came to me talking to him, and as usual, it was all about him.

John had a way about him that he always convinced me to forget about everything that had happened, and as always, I did. I don't think we ever got around to talking about what took place that night and how he wasn't at home with me and his children. I wanted to ask him where he had gone that night and who he had been with and who had told him the lies, but I knew he was the only one who had the right to ask questions, and that was just the way it was.

On his trial date, the young man dropped the charges, but the DA still tried to go after John. Somehow his appointed lawyer got the charges dropped down to a misdemeanor and six months on probation. He was also ordered not to go around the young man, which he chose to obey. The young man, of course, never came around our house again. Then life went back to our kind of normal, which meant more infidelity, lies, and me pushing everything back further into my heart.

I was so stressed out with life that I don't even remember going to the hospital to have my third child, which was a boy. I had to ask my family if John was there when the baby was born, and they had to tell me he was not. His mother had to bring him to the hospital. This was how I met her for the first time.

Through the help of my family, they prepared our room for me to bring Johnny home. He was named after his father, which was a curse thrown on him. But his smile was always infectious to everyone who met him.

I can remember how beautiful his little face was and how much joy he brought to my life, along with his older sister and brother. Between the three of them, they kept me busy and gave me no spare time to think about my problems.

CHAPTER 7

Help! There's No Way Out!

Within a few months after Johnny was born, I found out I was pregnant again with my fourth child, and tobacco season was over.

The landlord of the farm said he hated to do it, but he needed the land back because one of his children needed to move in, and they were going to raise the proper amount of tobacco for the coming year. There was nothing we could say, and Mom told him we would try to be out within thirty days. Normally when we needed somewhere to live, we would all take turns and drive different roads in search of anything that was livable.

Another house was found close by in the same town but off the mountain, and we all moved in. I always wondered whether my sisters and brother were scared to say they were tired of moving, but none of them ever did.

As the months passed, my belly grew bigger, and a heavy heap of depression grew inside of me as well. No matter what I tried, nothing seemed to ever stop John's wild streak. And his jealousy grew at a fast pace, which became more than I could bear. I walked on eggshells when he was around because I didn't want to make him mad or get slapped around.

Young men continued to come over all the time to see my sisters, and I tried to make myself invisible as much as possible. That was their company, not mine. But when they did come over, I would come out if John was there and talk, but I was scared to get too much into the conversation, for I knew his eyes followed every movement I made.

Young girls and women, when your husband or boyfriend is jealous like John was, it is about 99 percent true that they are cheating at every turn, and they want to make sure you don't give them payback. But what John didn't realize was that I wouldn't stoop that low and I thought more of myself. When I married him, I made an oath to God, and strangely, so did he.

There was the big church issue. Church never hurt anybody. The only thing it does is to get you to know God, get closer to God, or make you think about how you need to change for God.

I was raised that you always went to church unless you couldn't get there. I live by those same rules today. I was always in the choir or on the worship team. And if they needed someone to teach the kids, clean the church, or do anything where help was needed, I volunteered.

That was one issue we argued over a lot. He would go one Sunday, then miss three. When he did go, he'd play with the children and get one of them crying so he could volunteer to take them outside.

Because we sang at many churches, we heard many preachers preach on the subject of 2 Corinthians 6:14: "Do not be yoked together with unbelievers. For what do righteousness and wickedness have in common? Or what fellowship can light have with darkness?"(NIV). I had made sure that John received Christ as his Savior before we got married. I thought when you said you loved Jesus, you loved Jesus.

John seemed to never want to go with us to church anymore, and I eventually quit asking. I couldn't understand how a person who said he knew God could not like church or keep on doing the things he did. All I knew was that I faithfully loved God but didn't understand why He didn't step in and take my pain away.

I never knew when John would take off; he would be there one day working, and then the next day, he didn't come home. It was normally on payday, and the money he made was never spent on me or his kids.

As I look back at all the times John left us for days, sometimes months, my family had to always step up to the plate. They must have dreaded these days, for they all had to get together and figure out who would chip in to buy diapers, food, and milk for my children and me.

As the years progressed, I saw the disgust on their faces, and I became withdrawn and understood their disappointment in me. But we were family, and they always came to my rescue. I will never forget all they did for me. But at the same time, I felt my sanity start to lose ground.

I could also see the toil it took on my children because, without meaning to, the family would get angry at my children, especially the one named after him. When he would misbehave, they would say things like, "You're just like your father." I know my children paid the price for what all he did over and over.

As I waited for John to come home one Friday night, he didn't. Now I had three children and one on the way. Their ages were three, two, one, and the one to be born within a few months. I felt like I was ready for a nervous breakdown and felt there was no one I could talk to but God, and believe me, I did, but at this time in my life, I felt my conversation was one-sided. My thoughts were that maybe God was tired of dealing with my life, and I must be doing something wrong.

With a humble heart, I now know the only reason I'm here today is because of Him. But I wish I could have talked with someone I could look at and get feedback.

That is why I keep on repeating this: Please, if you're out there and can relate to this story, find a pastor, counselor, or person you can trust and talk with them, and believe me, God doesn't care if you do. Then ask for help to get away from the person doing you harm because, at some point, your mind might snap and you will have to pay the price.

Back to the story: After about 6 months, I found out that John had gone to the area where his mother lived. I usually found out where he eventually was because one of his sisters married my oldest brother, and she was always in contact with her family. I learned that John had met a girl and had moved in with her, but he never contacted me until right before I had our fourth child, which happened to be the day before he was born.

That day, John called me up and said he had seen the light. He wanted to live for the Lord and start over with the kids and me. He told me he loved us so much and expressed he didn't know why he always acted the way he did. Once again, I talked to Momma, and once again, she said she'd go and pick him up. As I look back, I wish my mother would have said no. I would have thanked her, maybe not at that moment, but in time, I would have.

I didn't know how to explain to my mother, but I told her I was having some problems with my body. After giving her the details, she explained that sometimes a woman's water would leak slowly instead of breaking all at once before a child was born, and I needed to be checked by my doctor.

We made a decision to go after John first, which was two hours away. The trip was like an "L," one hour west and one hour north. The doctor was in the middle of the point, which was in Lexington, Kentucky.

When we arrived at John's apartment, he came out and asked me not to come in because his girlfriend was in there, and he would bring out his stuff on his own. He also expressed he needed to go back and say goodbye for the last time because she was also hurting, and being the person I was, I said yes.

I wanted to see so much what she looked like. Was she prettier than me? Fatter than me? What did she have that I didn't? Why did he leave me? All these things ran through my mind as I sat there pregnant, waiting and wondering what was wrong with me.

I know you're thinking: was I stupid or what? The answer to your question is yes, but I didn't realize it at that time. The sad thing is that there are millions of young girls and women just like me doing the same thing, and that's why my story must be shared. God doesn't make no junk! Just remember that!

After picking him up and within a few minutes of him telling me what I wanted to hear, my tears flowed, and we made up. Mom butted in and explained that for precaution measures, we needed to stop by a hospital to make sure I was okay.

As soon as they examined me, I found out my water was leaking and had to be admitted. They said it could be very dangerous for the baby and me to have a dry birth, so I couldn't go anywhere, and they put me in a bed.

This trip had already been terrifying. It seemed like I couldn't have a normal birth experience, as I was always by myself, and John had to be found. This time I felt like God was punishing me for staying with John, but at the same time, I kept saying to myself, "You can't divorce him; it's wrong.

You're not praying enough for him. You're not a good wife, or he wouldn't be leaving you all the time." How many of you feel like that and question yourself all the time?

At around 11 p.m., I heard the nurse ask the doctor if she should give me a sleeping aid because of my exhausting, long day, and I heard the doctor tell her no because he was worried I would go into labor. As she left the room, the doctor turned to me and explained to me why he told her no. He said he didn't want me to have a dry birth and wanted me to go into labor the normal way, which would not be as dangerous for me or the baby.

At midnight, I still hadn't gone into labor and was still restless when the nurse came into the room and gave me a shot that I found out was a sleeping medicine, even though the doctor had told her not to. I remembered what he said and thought he must have changed his mind and told her to, but then I fell quickly to sleep.

Within the hour, I went into full labor, and it soon became a very dangerous delivery because I couldn't feel anything, and my body had shut down. They were trying to wake me up and explain to me what was happening, but the whole room was spinning, and I was in severe pain. I could see nurses and doctors working quickly, placing IVs in my arms, and chattering with each other, trying to figure out what to do. The nurse who gave me the shot entered the room, and the doctor got in her face and told her she was fired and to leave the room.

The nurses prepped me for a C-section, but out of the blue, my baby boy came forth without making a noise. I watched as the doctors did every kind of maneuver they could to bring life into my baby, but he was turning blue.

I could hear them as I came in and out, saying that the sleeping medicine had put my baby's brain to sleep. I was praying to God, "Don't take my baby," but after about twenty minutes, I heard one of the doctors say, "Let's try one more thing before we pronounce him dead." I wanted to cry but felt like I was dead and couldn't.

Then I saw one of the baby's doctors take my baby and said to the other baby doctor, "Let's play football." I watched as he bent over like he was getting into a position to hike a football, but the football was my baby boy. Then he placed my baby between his legs and said, "Hike." There went my baby, flying through the air until the other doctor caught him.

I was praying at this point, "Please God, let my baby breathe." As soon as the other doctor caught him, my baby started crying, and I as well, for he had already turned blue and was lying lifeless. I started waking up, and everyone in the room started laughing and shouting, "He's alive." We had all witnessed a miracle. That night I gave birth to another beautiful, healthy baby boy, who made baby number four, and his name was David. I thought of how David in the Bible had fought the Philistine, and my David had fought his Philistine.

After returning home from the hospital, things went back to normal, at least for a while. And once again, John was his good, repented self.

Within a couple of months of my child being born, I looked into a mirror and noticed a lump the size of a golf ball protruding out of the left side of my neck. I went to an old country doctor, and after examining me, he told me he was referring me to a specialist because he thought I had cancer and didn't know how to treat me. As I was taken home, I was ready to scream at the top of my lungs, "God, why?" I explained to God, "I am barely twenty-one, with four children who need me. I again asked God, "Please give me a miracle." Everybody was praying for me and told me that old doctor couldn't tell if I had cancer just by feeling my throat without further testing and to hold onto my faith in God.

A couple of weeks passed, and the golf ball-sized tumor had gotten a lot larger, so I went to the specialist. He ran some tests, and after being examined, the doctor walked out of the room and brought in a whole team of doctors. They sat down and agreed that after seeing the test results, they all believed I had cancer. But they said they would have to operate on me to find out if the tumor was malignant or benign. They needed to do the surgery as quickly as possible because the tumor was growing at a fast rate, and it had to be taken out. They said the growth had attached to one of my thyroid glands, and they scheduled me for surgery immediately.

With all the stress I had already experienced in my life, it took my brain just one step further into insanity. Here I was, twenty-one, with four children and a husband who didn't support me. I needed to scream help, but I didn't see a way out.

John was still on his best behavior, or I thought he was. It turns out the family spared me the truth and did not want to add to my worries.

The surgery went well, and they removed all the mass, took a biopsy, and told me it was cancer free, and God deserved another hallelujah from us all. The rest of my blessing was that I was able to care for my children very quickly. I was convinced there was a purpose for what I was going through, and God was the hero in all of this. Actually, I didn't recuperate that fast, but with that many children, once I could put one foot down on the floor, I was healed. What I didn't know was that even before the surgery; I was a couple of months pregnant.

After just a few months (you won't believe it), we all were headed back on the road again, which took us to California. After getting settled in, I went to a doctor and found out I was pregnant with baby number five. We had settled into an apartment, and John and I were getting along pretty good for five or six months, but once again, a decision was made, and all agreed to move again back to Kentucky (I do not remember who decided this, but it wasn't me), and I had only been twice to my doctor.

Even though my due date was within three weeks, and my doctor was against the move and said I should wait until I had the baby, I was scared to tell the family what he said, and nobody asked me. John and my family wanted to go, and the majority had ruled.

I think my two brother-laws were for moving back home because neither one of them had ever been out of Kentucky, and maybe they were homesick. When they discussed going back, my mom couldn't stand to think that her girls would be taken from her, so she would convince every one of us to go. California is pretty much a very busy state, nothing like those country towns.

I was pregnant when I left Kentucky with this coming child, and now I was eight months along with this coming child and now was leaving California. I remember talking to God and asking Him to change every-body's mind, but he didn't. If I could have taken my children and run away,

I would have, but where would I go? I had never had a job or driven a car. There was no way outta here.

We were on the road again, with five vehicles creating a convoy this time. John had taken an older van and made a bed in the back for the kids to sleep and play on. It would become our home for our four children and the one on the way.

The rest of the family vehicles included my stepdad and mom's vehicle, with my youngest sister and brother as passengers. Vehicle three belonged to my oldest brother and his family, along with my two sister's vehicles and their families.

I was so scared, being eight months pregnant thinking about what if I had to deliver this baby while on the road but I never opened my mouth back then and felt I had to do whatever I was told. I convinced my body I could handle it. My children needed me.

When we got there, money was tight, and we couldn't find a house, so we drove around till we found an old, abandoned house that was halfway falling down on one of the country roads. After looking it over, we discovered it had two rooms in the front part of the house that was livable. Everybody could move into the two rooms and make their beds on the floor but John, our children, and me. We decided to live in our van. We could still eat with everyone in the kitchen and then sleep in the van.

We made a decision to park close to the front of the house in the circle driveway. The drawback was that we had no bathroom, not even an out-house, so we turned an old out building that was a barn into a bathroom that stood about twenty-five yards from the house. This was quite a way for women to walk to go to the bathroom, especially after dark and especially a pregnant one to boot.

I admit sometimes when it was dark, and we girls were too scared to go that far to the barn, we would make the big tree near the side of the house our bathroom.

Then on one Sunday evening, after only being settled in for a couple of weeks, my water broke. The bad news was John was off fishing with my two brothers-in-law. But within an hour of them being gone, yep, my water had broken. Here we were, living in a van, with no house or bathroom. What more could a woman ask for? I broke down crying, but my sisters and mom quickly hugged and convinced me everything was going to be okay.

Meanwhile, my stepfather and brother were sent to find John to let him know it was time to go to the hospital. As soon as they got there, off we went to have baby number five at a hospital in the closest big city, which was fifty miles away. But I made it, and along came baby number five, born July 1976. We named him Jeremy.

While I was having Jeremy, my mom tried desperately to find a place for me to be able to bring the baby home to, but she couldn't find anywhere. I brought the baby home to the van and took very good care of him, even though we didn't have a house. But something was building up in side of me, and I didn't realize how mad I was. But divorce was off the table, for it was wrong, and who would help me out of this mess? There was no way out!

In a way, you can say we lived a life made for the movies. We did things that to some people were not believable, not even to me. We lived like a bunch of gypsies, always on the run.

The search for a house continued from July to October until the family finally succeeded in finding a place in Richmond, Kentucky, which was about twenty-five miles away. The place was an abandoned big building that, in time, had been called "The Poor House." It had been used for people who didn't have much money.

There was a main huge kitchen located in the main building, along with bathrooms and four or five apartments inside. Then there were two additional buildings, one on each side of the main building, but we didn't need them.

To this day, I don't know how my mom and family always found these places, but they did. And I can tell you we were pretty poor and needed a big place, and this one fit the bill. The vision was to remodel them into five huge apartments and one big, beautiful kitchen and living room. To our neighbors, I guess we looked like a cult that had moved in, but they could have taken the time to get to know us because the worst was yet to come.

All the men were in construction and knew how to remodel anything and did at night when they came home from work.

Within a week, the men quickly painted and fixed what needed fixing while the women cleaned till everything looked cozy as a home should be. Each family bought furniture to furnish their own apartment. Our apartment was finished first, equipped with baby beds and all.

As I looked around at the furnished and finished apartment, it felt pretty good compared to living in a van. It was good to have a place to finally bring my baby to. I started reminiscing how the place would look when completely done.

John and I had a bedroom that was enormous with a huge fireplace, and it was big enough to house all five kids, myself, and him.

The next week was a busy one for everybody, finishing all the touches to make it into five beautiful apartments. We all had our own spaces, which were very nice, yet we all lived under one roof and shared one huge kitchen. The good part about it on any given night was that if I didn't like what I was cooking, I would go to one of the other tables and sit down and eat meals that ranged from chili dogs, fried chicken, tacos, or pork chops. By the way, all the girls had been taught to cook, and the food was some of the best.

After living there close to a month, the cool weather started to set in. We hadn't used the fireplaces but assumed we needed to start. John went and got some wood and made a fire in our fireplace to cozy it up for the night, but I guess no one had told him fireplaces have a flue pipe that needed to be open when used.

I don't know if he forgot or just didn't know, but only by the grace of God we did not die that night because the flue pipe was closed, and soot filled the whole room and settled on everything, including us. God spared us because we could have died while in our sleep with all the smoke we inhaled.

When I woke up the next morning, all I could do was laugh when I opened my eyes. As I looked over at John (who was Caucasian), he looked completely black except for his white teeth. Our whole room was covered with a blanket of soot. Each child was black from head to toe, even my snow-white blanket.

I ran out to tell the others, and each laughed as they entered the room. Even John had to laugh, which was rarely seen.

That day was a day to remember, and the whole family helped us. For two days straight, the clean-up process happened. We had to wash everything and use a chemical that removed the smoke smell, and it took using a little capsize of bleach to put in our bath waters to clean the pores of our skin. I thank God for my mom and sisters who helped me clean up the mess.

Time moved on, and things seemed to go smoothly until one morning, after getting the men off to work, all of us girls sat down to drink coffee and take some time to relax and chat for a while before getting into our workload for the day.

We had not met many people of the neighborhood except at a little country store that was a couple of blocks away from the house. Of course, as all small towns in the east, questions were always asked like, "Where are yah from," and why we chose their town to live in.

But on this particular morning, we sat there, most of us still in our robes and gowns, when a knock came at the door. Upon opening it, there stood two policemen who said they needed to come in and ask us some questions. Once seated, they had a list of questions to ask us, things like our names, where we were from, and why we rented the place until what seemed like hours had passed, and the questions stopped. They had written all answers down on their notepad as we spoke.

One policeman continued to say it seemed like we were nice people, but he had a job to complete. When questioned what he meant by a job to complete, he stated that because we were from California, and all of us lived together and dressed differently from those in the neighborhood, the town had called a meeting. And in that meeting, over half of the community had signed a petition, then presented it to a judge to have us evicted.

He said they were scared and thought we might be like Charles Manson, which had happened five years before in California. My sisters and I did love maxi dresses (which looked like dresses gypsies wore, and my youngest brother did have long hair). Remember, we had just come from California a few months back.

At first, shock set in, and no one said a word till Mom did the talking for us, asking them why. They don't even know us; how could they bring such a judgment without notifying us? She asked if there was any way we could talk with them to change their minds, but he insisted it was too late, and he was there to enforce the law. We ask how long we had to get out, and he stated immediately. At this point, we all started crying, explaining to them the men were at work, and we had no cars and nowhere to go.

I think they felt sorry for us, so they said they would stretch the time to the next night at midnight. They both apologized again and left. Here we had just bought furniture to furnish the apartments, got settled, and now had to move again.

My new baby had gone home from the hospital to a van, then to a nice big home, and now we would be homeless again. How I longed to settle down and have my own home, but this would not be the time.

When the men arrived home, we broke the news to them, and anger set in. Mom calmed them down and told them we had to move fast and didn't have time to stay angry.

My stepdad called around to some builders he knew and explained what had just happened, and within a few hours, one of them said they had a huge house that was available behind the Red Mile horse racetrack. So off to moving we went again. Thank God, all the men were in construction.

CHAPTER 8

Breaker, Breaker,
What's Your Handle?

With one day to pack, rest or sleep for me was not in the picture. By nightfall, we completed the task and headed off to our new house. As soon as we pulled into the long driveway, I couldn't help but notice how beautiful the house was. It was in a rural area and set right behind the Red Mile, where the Kentucky Derby was held. If you looked over the back fence, you could see the horses. It was a huge two-story gorgeous home that belonged to one of the contractors my stepfather worked for. He explained they would be tearing the house down in the next twelve months or less, but for now, it was a nice house, and we could move in. As I look back, it is clear to see that God was caring for all of us, and it was a lot nicer than The Poor House.

Life began to slow down just a bit, and we seem to be comfortable in this house, which was very cozy and roomy for all of us.

One night after cooking, I was in the kitchen washing dishes. The babies were all asleep, and John had gone to the store to get cigarettes. I had started to notice he went to the store every evening around 10:30 or 11 p.m. and was gone for at least an hour or two. On this particular night, I was listening to the radio as I cleaned away at the mess in the kitchen. My passion was music, and every chance I got, I would listen and sing with the radio. Singing along with the radio made my chores go by very quickly. I knew every word to every song that came on.

Suddenly, I heard a woman's voice coming over the radio, saying, "Mudflap, are you there?" If you're from the middle seventies you probably remember how ham radios were the "in-thing," and everybody had what they called a handle. This was an ID name you used to identify yourself, something I guess like email, Facebook, Instagram, or Tic-Toc and other methods that are used today.

John's code name was "Mudflap." When listening to the radio and someone's ham radio was close, the airwaves would pick up their voices, and the radio sound would fade out. That night, my radio displayed a female voice, and my music went off as I clearly heard the woman ask for John's name. It had overpowered my radio and was no longer playing my music. Of course, when I heard his name, I quickly stopped to listen.

As she talked, my heart, like so many times before, started pounding, and my stomach became queasy. I listened as she continued her conversation after he answered, "I'm here," and continued with, "Where are we going to meet Friday night? and "Can you get away" He answered he'd figure out some excuse and meet with her as usual. He furthered stated that his wife was ignorant and would never figure it out. She ended with, "I miss you and will see you later," signed off, and he did too.

Past memories started rolling through my head of all the relationships he had embarked upon since the day of our marriage as well as all the ones I never knew about. Could this be happening again? Was there any way I could erase time and go back to right before catching him? My anger, hurt, and embarrassment welled up inside of me while my biggest fear was family, children, and friends finding out it was happening again.

At the same time, I struggled on thoughts of knowing he would be leaving again, and I would have to figure out how to support our five children on my own. I knew it was not the burden of my family, but they always had to take on the responsibility. I couldn't drive, so I had to be chauffeured everywhere. Nevertheless, I would not leave the subject alone. I rushed and told my mom and sisters to come quickly and listen to the radio to reassure myself that I wasn't hearing things. But confirmation immediately set in;

along with harsh words from each of them from the moment they heard the voices coming from the radio. The verdict: of course, it was him.

Mom placed her arms around me as well as my sisters to console me and quietly just said, "Let's see what happens when he comes home."

While I waited on him, I sat in the kitchen thinking back to a time in the past when I had to be taken to an emergency room. I had passed out in the bathroom that was attached to our room in this very house. Upon testing me for different things, the doctor came in the room and told me he needed to talk with me privately. John was also escorted to another room to be questioned as well. As I held my head down, his first question began with, "Do you have any additional sex partners?" Sitting there, I quickly exclaimed, "How can you even ask me such an awful disgusting question? I'm married and have never been with anybody else" (and at that same moment, I thought of the many women John had been with, but quietly kept it to myself).

After we were alone, the doctor related to me that I was a very sick young lady, and he had some very personal questions to ask me. You have to understand I was a very shy young lady, and it was hard for me to talk about sexual subjects, even to a doctor.

Just then, John, without warning, rushed through the door screaming at me, "Who have you been with?" knowing he was the guilty party. While crying, I just looked at him, thinking, "How can you say this to me? You are the only unfaithful one here, and you know it."

Soon, my mother entered the room, along with a nurse who just stared at John with an expression on her face that told him, "Tell another lie, and it will be the last lie you will ever tell." She was so angry, and he knew it, so he decided to leave the room and exited the building as well.

As everyone composed themselves, my mother held a conversation with the doctor, and he said he had seen enough to evaluate who the guilty party was. I was treated and released with a few medicines that he said would get rid of the infection, but I needed to take it all, and I did. Again, God cured me and took care of me.

Now thinking back, I thought about the woman I had heard on the radio and thought, "Could this be the woman he had been cheating with?"

Eleven-thirty rolled around, and here he walked in like nothing had ever happened, and life was as usual. He grabbed my hand and said, "Honey, let's go to bed."

As we passed the living room to get to the stairwell, I told my mom and sisters good night as we excused ourselves from the kitchen. As he and I were walking up the steps to our room, I thought of the Scripture where it speaks of people trying to act like lambs, but they are really nothing more than wolves in sheep's clothing.

As we entered our room, we could see the children were fast asleep, so I sat down on our couch. I quietly confronted him about what I had heard, but he had a unique way of convincing me it wasn't him. I quietly rolled over, feeling defeated, but couldn't stop the tears flowing from my eyes and hushed any sounds that wanted to come from my lips until I eventually cried myself to sleep.

The next morning, I acted like I was asleep as he left early to go to work. The pain filled my heart even more as I knew I had to face my sisters and mom. As I told them what he said, they quickly let me know they considered me weak-minded and made sure they addressed their opinions and then just left the room. They were getting fed up with him as much as I was. I just couldn't let them know.

Over the next few days, John acted as good as gold to take away all of my suspicions and made himself scarce from the view of my family. But after a week had passed, my Mom brought in a letter from the mailbox addressed to him but had a company's name on it. Mom told me to open it, for she suspected it was from a woman. I was scared to open it, but I did, and her thoughts were correct. The letter was from a woman he worked with, and she talked about how much she cared for him and couldn't wait until the day they would be together. Whether this was the woman, I don't know and I never asked or found out.

As I read the rest of the letter, my tears fell faster onto the pages, and I didn't know what to do. How could I be so blinded? How could the other woman be so blinded?

Why did he have such power over me? What made him tick? Why wasn't our relationship enough for him? All these questions and more haunted me and consumed my every thought.

I confronted him that evening, which seemed to last for hours. He finally got fed up with me because he knew I didn't believe his lies. But out of the blue, he picked up one of the children's toys and threw it at me. It hit me really hard right in the eye, which turned black quickly. That was when I shut up and gave up.

That night John knew he had to leave because the minute my family would look at my face, they'd come after him, so he left.

My family tried to stay out of our lives as much as they could, but they didn't want him to hurt me. He stayed gone for a week or more to give them time to cool down, then he came back. He always waited for a time when he thought the men would be gone to sneak into my room. And he was always broke. I wondered why he came back, but I assumed it was because the other women were treated the same why I was.

This was the pattern that I had become accustomed to, and it went on for years. Step one: John would come back begging (when he would run out of money), or he'd be kicked out and would tell me he loved me and that he would change, go to church, and then I would give in and take him back.

Step number two would be that after he came back, I would have to wait on him hand and foot. You see, he didn't want to face the rest of the family because he knew that they knew what the true story was.

He stayed cooped up in our room and had me cater all of his meals which made my work harder so it was like I had six children. Plus I would walk on eggshells to keep five children quiet because we still lived in one room.

Step three of the process would be that he always convinced me it was my fault, and I had to make it up to him. He said it was because we lived with my family. He said that's why he acted the way he did because I wouldn't move out. But the only time he ever wanted to move out was when he'd get back from one of his flings and we had no money. He'd say, "Let's go look for a house." Then I'd ask him, "What do we do for gas money to look for a house, and what do we rent it with? You have no job."

The only money we would have is where I would go apply for help and receive a welfare check or what my family had given me. I knew I would have to ask someone in the family if we could borrow some money for him to look for a job, or he'd start working on a job with my family again. The bottom line was when he had money, he didn't want to look for a house.

John always made good money, but I wasn't allowed to know what he made or ask him for any. It was his, and after he would buy his toys, such as remote airplanes or whatever, he would then give me a few hundred to use for our household. And one of my jobs was to make sure there was always milk in the house, not for the children, but for him.

Step four was the talk he gave me when he came home. First, it was nice to be with someone wholesome again. I always thought that was a compliment, but now when I think about what he said; I would just get angry and hurt and know what he was talking about. He always said, "You may be pretty and young, but nobody is ever going to want you because you have too many kids." In other words, he was reassuring me that he could come and go as he pleased, and there was nothing I could do about it.

Some months passed, and things settled down, but I knew in my heart I wanted a way out but didn't know how to do it. Meanwhile, we were on the road again, looking for a place to live where the story continues.

Once again, I address those of you out there right now as you are reading this story and thinking about the relationship you are involved with, whether it is a husband or boyfriend. How much does my story relate to you? Think about it. You're asking yourself if you are to blame and what you can do to fix the problem. The answer is, you're not at fault; your mate has the problem, and you can't fix it.

I urge you to get out and safely get the help you need. Your sanity and self-worth is at stake. Don't allow the enemy to keep you down. Find your strength, and don't allow the person controlling your life to drag you into theirs. You could do everything right, and it would not matter. Get out of the relationship and stand on solid ground.

There is a fact I must include in these words for you to understand the severity of your situation. I knew Jesus, and I was still making all the wrong decisions. But I will tell you if I had not known Jesus as my Savior, I know I would not have made it through.

John 14:6 says "I am the way and the truth and the life. No one comes to the Father except through me" (NIV). He is your true friend and will always be there for you. If you ask Him into your heart right at this moment, He will. And He will never leave nor forsake you.

As more months passed, and things settled down, the urge grew stronger in my heart to find a way out of this mess but I ask myself, how? The rage inside of me was growing with leaps and bounds. I had to think of a way out. I was getting desperate. You must understand I had to stay alert because my children were my first priority and I only had a few moments to think. But then reality would step in and I had to pull myself together.

Meanwhile, we had only taken the property till we could find another place to live, so the hunt was on. As usual, John was restless, and before I knew it, when the weekend came around, as soon as he got paid, he disappeared and didn't come home.

CHAPTER 9

Ride of Terror

Mom and us girls kept looking for a house, and after eight months had passed, we found one in the early fall in the country that was ready for move-in. Within that eight months John left again but I don't remember when. After a person is gone so much and my mind locked out so much all I can tell you is everybody had to pitch in to help me move my stuff, and it all had to fit into one room, which was the biggest room in the house. The room was big enough for me to fit two sets of bunk beds, along with a baby bed and a full-size bed for me. But I also had enough room to make a small living room with a beautiful red couch, end tables, and a coffee table, which made it look like a small bachelor's apartment.

After making the room comfortable for the kids and me, it started getting a little chilly outside, so we had to make sure there was enough blankets and quilts for us to stay warm. There was no central heat, but I did have a small space heater and an electric blanket. So with November around the corner, I hung thick blankets up on the backside of one of the bunkbeds as well as each end of the bed and took the top of the other bunk bed and pushed it beside the other. I also had a thick pair of curtains that slanted down like a tent. With that completed, I placed the space heater in the front so the children would be warm and cozy at night. The tent housed the three boys while my daughter, the baby, and I slept in the full bed with the electric blanket.

What we all didn't know was that the roof over my bedroom was not very stable. So when the first snowstorm came, we woke up to snow all over my couch, and you could see the sun coming through my ceiling. Here it was now early December, and the guys all had to fix the roof as quickly as possible.

John stayed gone till early spring, and then his mother brought him home and convinced us he needed to stay and take care of his children. I believe my family didn't want him to come back, and neither did I, but thought that it would take some of the load off of the rest of the family.

I don't even remember how we started talking to each other, but I can tell you that he played the four-step game I talked about in the last chapter, and we moved on. Somehow we managed to get along as well as the rest of the family.

There was my stepfather and mother, two sisters who were married, along with their husbands, and my oldest brother and his wife. There also were their four children altogether. I can tell you that Mom didn't want any of us to leave, but our families were growing, and we started talking about each family moving out, which happened a few years later. But what about me, how was that ever going to happen?

I remember we were getting along again pretty well until one late spring afternoon, John was riding his motorcycle back on the farm, and our kids were playing outside while I was watching them. He would take turns giving them rides on the dirt road that was on our farm. They were having so much fun.

Suddenly, John pulled up beside me and said, "Get on the motorcycle and ride with me. I have always been afraid of motorcycles and did not want to ever ride one. I also did not feel like it was ladylike and said, "No thank you, but I don't want to." Well that was the wrong thing for me to do. He kept on pressuring me to ride with him, and I tried so hard to tell him to just let me be and ride with the children. I explained to him I was scared. As we went back and forth, I could see his anger rising until the deal changed. Then he said, "Now you will ride it without me. You don't have a reason to be scared, and you will get over it." But I just couldn't.

His anger was at a boiling point, and he gave me a look that I knew I didn't have a choice. Trembling, I told him I had never rode and didn't know how, but at that point, I knew he didn't care, and I knew I had to ride. I continued begging him to stop forcing me, but his body pushed me upon the bike. He proceeded to give me a quick five-minute lesson and then said to go.

I thought I did what John told me to do and started revving the handle bars, but off I went, going too fast. With tears flowing down my face, I felt like I was in a horror movie, and there was no exit. I couldn't even remember how to slow it down. The bike went out from under me, and I hit the ground. As I looked up, I saw the bike going until it came to the barn and kept going straight up the side of the barn until it did a complete flip-flop and blew up in the air.

I quickly decided it was a good time for me to run as fast as I could and find a place to hide in the back of the farm because after the shock was gone, I knew John would be coming for me.

I really don't know for how long I hid, but I hid what seemed to be a few hours untill some of my family came and found me, and they had cooled John down and told him he'd better not touch me. My brother and brothers-in-law told him they would handle him if he didn't. He got the picture and never commanded me to ride another motor cycle again. I think about it now and can laugh about it, but it wasn't so funny back then.

Some months passed, and things settled down, but anger began to rise with in my spirit. It became harder to forgive John and accept that I had to stay in the same house with him. For the children's sake and my sanity, I buried it deep within my soul. My heart wanted to run away, but that was becoming more and more of a dream. I was thankful to have my mom and sisters around because they would allow me to have a few moment to catch my breath make me laugh some. John always found a way to get out of being a father or husband by going fishing, hunting or fixing someone's vehicle. But he never took one of our children with him.

I knew that I was to stay as close to my family as possible because that is where I felt safe.

I feel like I am playing a broken record but it wasn't long until we were on the road again to California, where my story continues.

CHAPTER 10

Two Dozen Yellow Roses

I had not been pregnant for almost two years and for the first time since we had been married, I didn't look like a pumpkin. It was nice to not wear maternity clothes and start losing weight. My body had begun to heal, physically and mentally, and I finally had come to the terms that I was an obedient wife and that meant there were many rules for me, but none for him, yet I actually thought this is how God wanted me to be.

After arriving back to California, for the first time, we quickly found a house and moved into it by ourselves in a horse town call Norco. John found a good job with someone he knew and went to work within the first few weeks.

But after just a few months, John started playing the same story out again just as soon as the bills came due. I thought now this would be his chance to prove that we could make it on our own, and his excuse of why he always left would be gone. As usual, I only received a small portion of what he made and knew it was against the rules to ask him how much he made. Money problems always seemed to be part of our worst arguments, and I tried so hard not to say anything, but I didn't want to move again, and the children needed a place to call their home. Yet, the bills were due, and John had offered no money. Getting enough money to pay for our rent, utilities, and food was something I always had to beg for.

From what I had investigated, at my own risk, those should have been covered easily with about 25 percent of what he brought home. But I had to accept the wild tales he would tell me and drop the argument for the sake of the consequences that would follow if I didn't. But John always had plenty of money to buy his hobbies or go on his trips, and I knew his tales were just lies.

But I paid what I could and stayed quiet. I found myself actually asking God to help me find the money another way. Do you think he did, and was it right that I asked Him? The answers were no, he didn't, and I didn't have the right to ask Him.

We kept on just getting by in our marriage and trying to act like we loved each other, but it got harder for me to act like nothing was wrong, but I played along. I will say that we barely existed because we never really got along. At the same time, there was a longing inside of me that really wanted to be part of John's life with no secrets, but I thought, "What could I do to make it happen?"

Soon after moving in, I found out I was pregnant with baby number six, and I hated to break the news to John, but I had to figure out a plan to tell him. I decided to break the news to him after we had come home from church on a Sunday night. I knew he wouldn't like it, but I didn't expect him to react the way that he did. He had not physically hit me for over a year, and it felt good. The children had gone to sleep, and this seemed like a good place away from them for me to let him know.

That night, John broke his record. When I broke the news, he immediately exploded, and his fist entered the dining room wall. Then after calling me all his choice of names, he abruptly stopped and told me I had to get an abortion. His words were, "Everybody is doing it," and he didn't need another mouth to feed or take care of. I wanted so badly to rebuttal his words and ask him, "*When* you take care of them," but I knew better and just said it in my mind. I told him I was not like everyone else and would not abort my baby. It took everything inside of me to stand up to him, but I told him no matter the cost, I would not.

That cost was high, and the beating began. John would start accusing me of acting like I was better than him and tell me I was no better than him. With each of his sick remarks, another blow would come my way. He thought if he hit me enough, I would give in. But he actually knew if it was something that went against what Jesus taught, I would not do it, even to death.

It seemed like the beating would not end, but the blows finally stopped, and I just lay on the floor. I thanked God that none of the children had woken up. John stomped out of the room and went on to bed, which was a blessing for me. I finally had the strength to sit up and compose myself and slowly made my way into the bathroom. At least all the bruising could be hidden except for one black eye.

It seemed like he always knew just where to hit me so it couldn't be seen to the naked eye, but this black eye would. I didn't want anyone to know, so I decided not to go anywhere for a few days until I could cover it up with makeup.

The next morning, one of my sons asked me what happened to my eye, and I told him I ran into the door, and he believed me. I made sure I didn't go around anyone or invite anyone over for a few days till the bruising started turning yellow. By the end of the week, I could cover the black eye with enough makeup.

The next night, I made sure when John came home from work, his dinner was on the table, and that calmed him down some. The next night, which was Friday, to my surprise, he actually came home and placed a huge vase in the middle of our dining table filled with two dozen of the most beautiful yellow roses I had ever seen. I knew even though he didn't say it, this was his way of saying, "I'm sorry." He talked to me and told me I didn't have to get an abortion (which I wasn't going to anyway), but at least he agreed with me.

Things calmed down, and no one ever knew about the beating but me, him, and the Lord, who saw everything.

When my mother and sisters came by the next day, I showed the flowers to them and just told them how wonderful John was. One of my sisters asked why he bought them, but I told them he just bought them for me out of the blue because he loved me. I lied to them and lied to myself. They didn't say anything, but years later told me they figured something had happened.

As I write this now, I ask myself how a vase of flowers could change my attitude toward him so quickly. Yet I can't answer that question for you, but

I ask you the same question right now: if you're going through a similar situation, what is your answer? Again, I tell you to seek help and get out until he gets help or before you get hurt.

I consider myself to be one of the blessed ones because I never landed in a hospital because of his physical abuse. Or maybe I'm thankful that I am alive and well. I give thanks to God for sparing me and watching over me.

The good part of this story is that seven months later, I gave birth to a gorgeous baby boy who had the most beautiful white hair and bright blue eyes. He would be the last boy of five that I would have. Somehow, he was the only child I had who was actually born in California. I loved him at first sight. I don't think it matters how many children you have; each one is a blessing and a miracle from God in their own way.

I can end this chapter by letting you know we actually moved again to another house in California, but within a few months, we were back in Kentucky again. I got tired of moving, and my sisters and brothers said they did too, so I don't know who was to blame. I guess different ones at different times had the urge. But the urge never came from me. Every time someone wanted to move back to Kentucky or California, we all had to agree unanimously, and after some heavy negotiating, we all packed up and went.

CHAPTER 11

Where the Deer and the
Roaches Will Play

This time we moved to the outskirts of a small country town named Cynthiana, Kentucky. It was a town that my auntie had lived in for years and told us about a place that she knew for rent. For a house being in the country, this house was beautiful, inside and out. While being shown the home, one of the things that stood out to me was a large trash can filled with numerous empty cans of Raid. I asked the owners if the house had a problem with bugs, but they assured us they had sprayed it just in case, and they had never had a problem.

The house was very clean and had a very nice big bathroom next to the kitchen, along with one master bedroom downstairs and two big bedrooms upstairs. When we got through looking at the inside, we walked outside and walked around the house, and I noticed a stairwell on the outside of the house that led up to a private door. I asked if that door went into part of the house upstairs and was told it was just a storage part that was separated from the rest of the house, and the owners used it for storage. They also said that there was no entrance on the inside of the house. I told them I was ok as long as no one lived up there. Of course, we rented it, and I thought it was such a cute three-bedroom ranch-style home with no problems.

After renting it, we moved, in with the help of my family and worked hard for hours till we all couldn't work anymore and decided to settle in for the night. We were so tired getting all the furniture carried in and placed in the right rooms that we decided we would quit working after setting up the children's beds.

I had them get dressed for bed while I placed sheets and blankets on each of their beds. I kissed and tucked each of them in, and before I turned the lights off, they were sound asleep.

By the time I got downstairs to our bedroom, I just wanted to sleep myself. John had laid down the box spring and mattress only, so I said, "That's it," and flopped down on the bed to get some sleep, and the lights went out. But sleep didn't come. Have you ever been so tired that you couldn't fall asleep? Well, this was that kind of night.

As soon as the lights went out, I felt something fall on my face but quickly knocked it off and turned back over, trying to go to sleep. Within minutes, I was squirming in the darkness, feeling like things were crawling on me when John asked me if I felt like things were crawling on me, and I said yes. After a few minutes, he decided to get up and turn on the light. And all I remember was jumping up and down while wiggling and screaming at the top of my lungs and knocking things off of my whole body. As soon as the light came on, we looked up to the ceiling and discovered our ceiling and walls were covered with black blankets of roaches. I had never seen anything like that to this day, nor do I ever want to experience anything like that again. We ran upstairs, gathered the kids, and placed them into our car, and off we went to rent a motel room. We contacted the owner, who said she didn't know the house was infested and would hire an exterminator company. When they came out, the man said he had never seen a house that bad. The house was tented for a whole month, and then we moved back in. I would like to tell you my story was always laid back, but I can't do that.

After getting settled into our new house for a few months, one of John's brothers came down to see us, and they decided to go hunting. He and John loved to hunt, fish, or anything else that had to do with the outdoors. The problem was that it wasn't hunting season.

While writing this part of the story, I think of some of the things I have had to do while I was married to him, and it makes me quiver. There were times when we would go hunting in the car at night with all the kids. And even though I didn't have a license and barely knew how to keep a car on the road John would tell me to drive. He would insist that nobody was on the country roads at this time of the night and I just had to go slow. As I drove he would sit in the passenger's seat with his rifle, flashlight, and head sticking out the window. I hated the sound of a gun shooting out of our car while our children were present. And I can tell you it was under duress. Also, I have cooked rabbit, possum, squirrel, black bird, frog legs, snake, deer, and a few other things but I wish I could have said no but I did what I was told. If they could be caught, I had to cook them. That's why this part of the story needs to be told.

I know every bite of meat we eat comes from killing the animals, and I love meat, but there is a reason there is seasonal hunting for different animals, but John wasn't very good at following rules. I think there are rules in place as well as how things are supposed to be done.

As they talked, they both decided to go hunting anyway, and if they shot a deer, they would use precaution. After finding and shooting a deer, they decided to leave the deer behind in the forest, as they didn't want to get caught by the game warden, and they would leave it to drain all the blood back in the woods. They roped and tied the legs of the deer and hung the deer upside-down upon a huge tree branch so the blood could drain and left him in the woods for a whole day and night. They knew they would have to bring it to the house after dark for fear of being seen in the daylight.

Think about this part of the story as you read it. What if you were me and the next night they came into my house dragging a dead, skinned deer across my floors and pushed him into my bathtub? When I saw it, I became physically sick to my stomach. I watched as a trail of blood made a path to my clean bathroom. Thank God, we had linoleum rugs on our floors. I knew that once they got finished, I would be the cleanup crew and wished I didn't have to be part of it. But I knew the job was mine and didn't have a choice in the matter. As I came to view what I needed to do to clean up, the smell was horrific. They told me they had never cleaned one before and convinced me that was probably what it was supposed to smell like before cooking. They cut it into roast, steaks, and much more and then they wrapped it up with brown packaging paper and tape.

After they finished, it took me a few hours to disinfect my floors and bathroom to get them back in use, but I survived through it all.

I am not against killing your own animals for food and processing everything, but the way they did things were illegal, and I shouldn't have had to participate if I didn't want to. And they should not have done it in my house the way they did.

After all the meat went into our freezer, they left out a small portion for me to cook. As I started cooking the meat, the aroma that traveled through the house smelled so bad that John and his brother came into the kitchen to taste their prized catch. But upon their taste test and to their amazement, they found out the meat was really rotten, and I wasn't forced to try it.

John quickly ran toward the bathroom as he became sicker by the second to empty out his stomach while his brother was not too far behind. After things settled down, they figured out that the rest of the meat they had put in the freezer was probably just as rotten. They talked between themselves and figured out what had happened. It was summertime, and it was not a good idea to leave it in the woods overnight to drain. All their work was in vain. I wanted to tell them if they had obeyed the law, it wouldn't have happened, but I didn't. At this point, I felt sorry for them. Now I can laugh about it. But life does move on, and lessons are learned.

CHAPTER 12

Pregnant Again

We moved to a place where my last child was born. It was a very pretty place where the beautiful house sat back off the road, where weeping willow trees lined the driveway. I don't remember when John left this time; all I know is he left right after I became pregnant with our last baby. As usual, his pattern was I would get pregnant, and he would leave till right before time for me to have the baby. It became a ritual, and this time was no different.

Even though this was a picture-perfect Southern-style four-bedroom, two-story house, there was one drawback. At this house, we didn't have running water except in a downstairs kitchen sink, which had a hand pump with cold water only. So for baths, I would heat water on the stove and fill up two five-gallon drywall buckets and then carry them upstairs, where I had a huge wash tub that I gave the kids a bath in. Then I had gallon jugs of warm water, so as I washed each child, I would stand them up in the tub, and when done, I would pour the gallon of water over them, starting with their hair, to rinse them off. Next, the water would be thrown out the window, and I would repeat the pattern with each child.

When John did come back, he didn't even offer to help me carry the water up the steps. One night when I told him how tired I was and asked if he could help me, his reply was, "Maybe you'll lose the baby if you carry enough water; I'm tired too." I never asked him again.

With this last pregnancy, I had quite a few problems. The baby lay on my bladder for the last four months of my pregnancy, and I had to drag my right leg to walk, but I knew I'd make it, and I did. It seemed as if the entire burden always lay on me. I became immune to my feelings and eventually kept them deep inside, for it was easier to be a robot.

The day finally came, and I was so glad to give birth one more time to a beautiful baby girl. I had one girl, then five boys, and now the end pregnancy was another girl. Here name was Jennifer, and like Ricky, she had beautiful white hair and the most beautiful blue eyes. People talked about how beautiful she was every time I took her out. I felt on top of the world to be blessed with all healthy beautiful children but sad at the same time because the feeling wasn't the same from their dad.

I knew something was wrong with this pregnancy, and so I told them after having her that I needed to have my tubes tied or fixed, for something was wrong and had been wrong, but I didn't know what it was. They scheduled me for a procedure that was only supposed to be a thirty-minute operation. It turned out to be a two-hour operation because there were some major problems, and they said I could have never gotten pregnant again. The day came, and I went home with my lovely baby girl.

Not long after her birth, John left again, and my family decided to move back to California. I really didn't want to go, but I didn't have much of a choice. I had to take just enough to make it on because I didn't even have a way to go; I couldn't drive and didn't have a car. I had to figure out which kid was riding in what car and with whom. My children were spread out among three cars. I rode in my mom's car with the three youngest. The whole way, each time we stopped, I had to listen to all the complaints of how the children were rowdy and wouldn't mind themselves. I didn't have much to say about anything, so it was like my kids were up for grabs. I had to get to California, and I knew I was blessed to have a family that took me along. They probably were frustrated as much as I was. But at least we really loved each other.

There was never a part of the ride that I didn't have at least one child or two on my lap. Many times my legs went to sleep, but I didn't complain. I kept so many feelings to myself that nobody ever knew. There was just so much to address.

At night where ever we stopped, I had an old tent I had brought with me for the children and me to sleep in. It usually wasn't bad, for I made their experience a good one and told them we were camping out. The boys were very much excited about that. But one night, it poured down rain in Texas. We had stopped at a rest area, and the men had pitched our tent up in a grassy area. During the night, it rained harder. The tent began to leak, and one by one, I pulled the kids in closer till the dark early hours of the morning when the whole tent was flooded.

I hated to bother my mom, but I had to knock on their car window to see if we could get in. We were all drenched. It was about four in the morning. Of course, she let us in. Soon the rain stopped, and we all changed clothes and headed on toward California. The next day, we drove till we reached the state line.

I think one of the hardest parts about moving a lot was settling in. When we arrived in California, we all moved into one place till an old friend helped me get a place of my own for the first time. He knew my mom and stepdad. My stepfather had contracted a lot of work from him and had sold him their house the last time we had moved to Kentucky.

John had been gone for quite a while, and I had started feeling good about myself. I had tried to move on with my life. Yes, I was on welfare, but I knew how to manage my money and pay what my bills were. I went back to school to get my GED, for I hated being on public assistance and wanted to get off of it. It seemed for the first time in my life, I had worth. I had become independent. The bills were getting paid, plus I had a little left over. I had control over the kids in a good way, and best of all, there was peace in our home.

Well, this family friend owned quite a few homes, and asked if I would like to rent one of them. It was a nice four-bedroom home in a very good neighborhood and close to all my family. He even came over a lot to make sure there was nothing I needed. He brought me things I could use to help me get on my feet. As I look back, he had known my family for years and knew John and how I was treated.

But he was just a very good friend.

You would think I would never want John back around, and I didn't want him back. I think he knew that, so this time he called my stepfather instead of me. He convinced them I needed him, and he needed me. He worked his spell on them, and they started working on me. They would say things like I was not going to be able to handle the boys as they got older, so I needed John around.

Finally, I came around. I wish I had never listened to them, for they were wrong. They didn't like John, and now he had hypnotized them to persuade me.

Finally, I gave in and let John come home. My feelings had really changed toward him, but I did it anyway. My anger and hatred had built up for John, and I wanted to stay away from him. My life had started turning around, and God had given me back my self-worth. But I thought maybe God wanted me to help him, and I was married to him, so maybe he had changed. We'd see.

Things went okay, but I just wasn't the same. What I had thought was going better I found out many years later just how bad things were from stories my children told at holiday dinners. He didn't leave, and we didn't argue as much, but little did I know, some of the things I learned would make the hairs stand on your chest, as the old saying goes. So I will tell you one of these stories because it will show you how the person you marry and live with can change the lives of even your children.

One story they told me was when I went to the grocery store, and he stayed home and watched the children. They all said something of his was missing, so he lined them all up in the garage and told them he would whip them one by one and continue the cycle till somebody confessed. They said one of them finally confessed so he would stop whipping them. They said he had put it up himself, and it wasn't even missing.

On this same occasion, they said John took one of the baby kittens they had and told them if they ever lied again to him he would do to them what he was going to do to the kitten. Then he took the kitten and wrung his neck off in front of all of them. I can look back and remember finding the kitten, but nobody ever told me what happened, but I always wondered.

He told me an animal must have gotten to the kitten. The kids never said a word, and I was not aware of the things going on. I really thought he was handling himself better. His temper rages seemed to be less but little did I know his drug habit was getting worse.

In the last year of living in this house, his brother and sister-in-law came out and settled in the area we lived in. His sister-in-law would come over and tell me I needed to learn to drive. But every time I mentioned the subject, it got rerouted. One day when John was being picked up for worked, she convinced me to go with her and learn to drive. He had an extra set of keys in a drawer, so access was available. After about a week, I had driving down pretty much but didn't know how to tell him.

I soon found out I didn't have to, for my mom somehow told him, and on that day, he raged into the house, didn't say hi or anything, but with a pair of tin snips in his hands, he angrily went to the drawer where the extra keys were and took them out and cut them up. He started the conversation with, "What in the blanket-blank are you thinking? You can't drive." When I explained I had learned, he said, "Okay, if you know how you can, go down right now and pass the test; if you don't, you're in trouble."

We went down to the DMV, where I passed the written test with a 98 percent and the driving test with a 96 percent. When we were through, he stated the only reason I passed was because the instructor was a woman. Nevertheless, I gained some freedom that day, even though I was thirty years old. It felt good to know I wasn't stupid and could drive myself where I needed to go. I had been convinced I couldn't drive or do anything for myself without the help of someone.

After we had been at this same address for about two years, John and one of my brothers-in-law talked and made the decision that we were going back east again. They didn't like California, and John said we could finally settle down. I already had liked how I had settled down, but he was the boss. We sold everything, and I said goodbye for the first time without the whole family going. Mom assured me they would all be shortly behind us. So my younger sister, her husband, John, and I, along with all our children, made the journey back to Kentucky.

CHAPTER 13

Disaster Strikes

We found a house that was in a beautiful rural area and had four bedrooms on the ground floor, along with a finished full basement attached with an additional bedroom. It was a newer home that was all electric and located in a middle-class area where anybody would want to settle down. It was a very clean house within a quiet area, resting upon a beautiful piece of land. It wasn't in the city but close enough for comfort, a place where we made plans to buy it.

John had been on his best behavior, and I thought he was finally beginning to mature. We were getting older, and I was so tired of moving, which I had expressed to him.

Once we got settled, I enrolled the kids in school. All were in school but the youngest two. My sister and her husband settled within a few miles from us, which made it nice.

The rest of my family followed us to Kentucky the following month. The first who arrived were my youngest sister and her new husband, along with my youngest brother and his new wife. They had both recently gotten married in California, and neither of their spouses had ever been out of the state. My mom and stepdad had trailed along with them. While this group came to stay with us until they found a house, my oldest brother and sister and their families went to stay with the other sister who came with us. It was temporary until they found their own homes.

I placed my little brother and his wife in our basement bedroom, which was next to the family room and laundry room. There was a huge fireplace furnace centered in the family room that heated up the whole house. I placed my youngest sister and her husband in one of the four bedrooms and my mom and stepdad in our living room on a sofa bed. The three remaining bedrooms housed my children and John and me.

I was so happy I could pay back some of the generosity to my family that had been done for my children and me.

One morning when all the men had left for work and the children had left for school, my youngest two children were watching cartoons in my bedroom and arguing about which channel to watch. I went to change a channel on the television for my younger two to watch and was cooking some breakfast in the kitchen when I suddenly left the kitchen to go referee Rick and Jen in our bedroom.

Along the way back, someone in the living room asked me a question, and I got sidetracked from cooking. I needed to throw in that the night before the coil in my electric oven had sizzled, and sparks flew. But we thought it was okay. We turned the oven off. Being gone only a few minutes, we smelled smoke, and I ran back to the kitchen. The whole kitchen was aflame. The house was all electric, and had wires that ran up and down the walls in every room. The wires also were spread apart every two inches, which allowed the house to be heated. Apparently, this is what had caught fire. I was told by the firemen later that the night before had sparked the wires to smolder behind the oven, and when I turned on the burner the next morning, it set the fire in motion.

We had ordered a phone, but back then, it took a week or two for them to come out and install them, so we didn't have one. I gathered up the children and took them outside as my mom, sister, and sister-in-law made it out safely. Because it was below freezing, and there was a foot of snow on the ground, my mom took the kids next door, and even though they weren't home, they found the garage door unlocked. She pulled it up and placed the children inside, along with my pregnant sister. I ran down the street hollering till I found an old man five doors down who couldn't hear well. Somehow I had lost one of my house shoes in the snow but kept going. He called the fire department, but by the time they got there, almost an hour later, everything was gone except the outside redbrick.

When I finally got back up to where my house was, I found my mother had ran back in to get a bird they had left in the house and the cage had hit her head, and she had to have stitches.

I was standing with only a robe and gown on and one house shoe, and we had just lost everything. We all stood watching in horror as the firemen were still watering everything down. Finally, the fire had been put out, but everything was still smoldering. We had brought for the first time so many new things from Cali. My sister and sister-in-law had just lost all of their wedding gifts, along with their wedding gowns. As we all cried, we kept on saying that everything was gone. The feeling I had was nauseating. I just fell to the ground, thinking, "What are we are going to do?" We had just signed the papers to buy it two weeks before this.

We were all freezing to death, and I looked over at my pregnant, crying sister while my sister-in-law was crying in another area, and my mom tried to calm us all down. Other neighbors had come around and brought us blankets to place around our shoulders. Someone had gotten word to all the jobs our husbands were on, and they were on their way home to us.

Because we had so many children, I found out later someone had called the news channel, and they sent out camera crews from all the major networks. They ask me if they could film our children as they descended the bus when they arrived. I granted them permission but asked them to please not film me, for being in a robe and gown was not what I wanted people to see. An elderly woman had brought me some clothes to put on and gave me a pair of shoes that didn't fit, but I was appreciative of them, but I did not want to be seen on TV. The camera crews understood and respected my wishes.

As they mingled through all my family, the school bus suddenly arrived, and all cameras went toward them. The camera crews caught glimpses of each of their little faces as they got off the bus and witnessed how they had come home to see they had no home left. Little did the media realize as they filmed my children, this was just one more tragic event in their lives they would remember. I can still remember the looks on each of their faces, but I don't have words to describe it.

It was hard to fathom as I stood there watching the scene unfold that none of us had anything left. I called my other sister's house to let her know what had happened, and she said they would start preparing her house for all of us to bed down for the night, and she'd see us when we got done. Also the police contacted John, my stepdad, brother, and brothers-in-law at their jobs as well as the schools where my children attended. What were we going to do?

When John arrived, he gladly accepted the invitation to be interviewed and took center stage for all of us. I believe his words were what he had didn't matter as long as his kids were taken care.

In my mind, I was asking myself, "Does disaster always have to follow me?" But, as I was pondering all of these feelings, my eyes quickly glanced over to my mom as a paramedic attended to the cut on her forehead. I rushed over to give her a big hug and told her everything would be alright. Then I walked around to check on the rest of my family as they had encountered the same disaster as me.

Reality suddenly rushed back in when neighbors stepped up and assured me there was help on the way and not to worry, for we would get through this. They assured me they were rapidly working behind the scenes with the news media and neighbors arranging help for us.

The television stations agreed to run clips twice a day for a week with drop-off places that viewers could donate items for us to receive. The gifts ranged from furniture, clothing, dishes, money, and so much more. I was overwhelmed by the generosity of others. We had more than enough.

I found out later one of the owners of our house owned the neighborhood country store, and the old man where I had used his phone to call the fire department was her brother. They all set up posts at their stores and other places for people to start dropping off items to help us all. Everything was arranged without our help. We all knew God had supplied our needs and more.

As I think back to each of their births, my children had been through so much in their young lives. Back then, I never thought about what damage they went through, thinking it didn't hurt them like it did me because they were so young. But I can tell you by the stories they reminisce about on holidays when we're all together, their stories are horrid, and each of them has been damaged profusely. But God is a faithful God, He never left us, and it is work, but He is dealing with each of us.

For those of you who are reading this and are going through similar circumstances, just remember if you have children, what you are going through, so are they. God doesn't want His little ones to go through this kind of life.

The Red Cross was called in, and they placed us in a temporary five-bedroom trailer until we could find a new home. I will never forget the kindness of people who gave to us in many ways. We were well taken care of.

To end this chapter with some good news, after a few days, we went back to our burned home, and as we were going through the rubble, we found in my bedroom the big box that held all of my pictures and memories that had not been touched by the fire. The outer layers were burnt on all four sides, but the middle was not, and God had protected all of them. That was a miracle God had given me. And my youngest son had found his Mr. Bim Zippy stuffed monkey that he loved so much. It was barely scorched on his forehead. He has that monkey to this day.

CHAPTER 14

Trick or Treat, Kick Him with My Feet

After the fire, we moved to a nearby city not far from where we had lived. With all the help of friends and strangers, we were able to get back on our feet. It was the first time in quite a while that John had seemed like he had really started changing.

The house was a Southern-style home that had all the comforts. There were five bedrooms, three baths, a huge formal dining room, and even a screened-in back porch with a bathroom that had a shower. The outside was just as gorgeous with porches on every side, you know, the kind of porch you would sit on and enjoy a nice cold glass of sweet Southern tea.

The house sat a mile back off the main road. The good part was that the driveway was not gravel but a blacktop road. I enjoyed driving back to get to the house because the scenery was so gorgeous to look at. We even had a few acres, and the kids would go back to a creek and swim, or they could roam the fields until dark. It was a life that you escaped into and got used to. It was peaceful, and family could come over and enjoy it with us. It seemed like everything was going so well; John even had a good job, and we paid the bills. Months had passed, and we were living the good life as far as monetarily, but little did I know things were about to change.

John's attitude did not change, and over the last few years, we had grown more apart just existing, with no love between us. I was always on my guard, waiting for the next dangerous move to happen.

But the house did create a place for me to enjoy the children and appreciate the life that God had given me. I was still married, had seven beautiful kids, and went to church on Sunday and Wednesday Night Bible study, but was still very much alone and wanted our marriage to include love, but it didn't. I tried to give the children the appearance that life was normal as well as creating a persona to my family and those who knew me, but I didn't realize that I was going down a deep dark road that wouldn't end well.

I had no one to talk with and didn't realize I could have talked with God, but at this point in time, I didn't even have a close relationship with Him. I knew I loved Jesus and had accepted Him into my heart as my Savior, but diving deeper into depression over the years, I had stopped talking with Him. He hadn't shut me out; I had slowly shut Him out without realizing it. I allowed myself to pull away from the one who loved me with open arms and had opened a door for Satan to play with my mind; I can't believe it as I write this, but when my children would go to school, I would find myself going to a library and finding a book that talked about different ways to kill a person without leaving a trail of evidence behind. I was desperate to get out of this mess I had placed myself in. I didn't believe in divorce, but I was actually thinking that if I murdered him without people knowing I murdered him, it was not a sin. It sounds like I was losing my mind, and I guess I was. I wonder how I forgot about the sixth commandment. But I did.

Now this is a part of my story you must read with caution; it will sound like a Halloween movie, but it's not. It was real life, not a play that gets watched, and then you walk out, and it's over. It's how the devil creeps into our minds and tries to justify sin, telling you it's okay to kill, that he or she deserves death.

It was a breezy, chilly Halloween night in 1982. We had moved out in the country, into a two-story farmhouse. The house was nice and had plenty of room for a big family like ours. I was thankful the Lord had blessed us. The rough part was that we didn't have a phone, and we lived a mile back off of the main highway. The driveway was blacktop and curved back and forth and ended in front of our house but parted off to the side of the house and went on to pass the rest of the farm.

The kids had come home from school excited about going trick or treating, for we had planned as soon as their father got home from work, we'd head to the city (this plan had been Okayed by him). I fed the children and placed John's in the oven to keep it warm. I don't even remember what I had cooked, but it really doesn't matter. Does it? As soon as they ate, they rushed up to their bedrooms to get ready for the big night. I had laid out each of their costumes in each of their rooms.

I had been making their costumes all day while they were at school, and I'll admit I was not a designer, but the kids didn't seem to mind or ever act like they did. I think they were always just glad to experience every moment of happiness they could. With all the circumstances they went through, they held up pretty good. I realize now that the Holy Spirit had angels that protected us. In His word, He says, "I will never leave nor forsake you." And I can honestly say that He never did.

John normally came home around six or six-thirty. As usual, if he was a few minutes late, I would start to worry. It was almost pitch dark, and the kids were waiting anxiously, squirming in their costumes. As it was now nearing seven, my stomach begin to hurt and my heart began to flutter very fast; this was normal for me. First, I would wonder if he had been in a wreck, or if he had taken off and left us stranded again like he had done so many times before, or if he was coming home drunk and high.

Even though the kids never said anything, I can remember seeing the same fear in their eyes so many times, but I didn't realize it then; I was too caught up in my own fear. I didn't think it bothered them; how wrong I was. Are you in the same denial? Think about it.

Then came seven-thirty, and the anticipation starting to leave the children little by little, with them asking the question, "Mom aren't we going," but as usual, I started making excuses as I had done for the past eleven years and would continue to do for the next four.

Then the sounds I had not wanted to hear came. Out in the country, you could hear the sounds afar off, the sound of a car screeching and sounding like it almost missed the driveway. As I looked at their faces, the fear was there; we knew who it was. In a split second, the older kids stated running in different directions while we listened to the screeching of the tires as he came flying down the curved drive.

Later, I found out the boys had gone to the roof to hide and my oldest daughter to her room. One of the boys heard my youngest daughter and climbed back into the house and grabbed her and climbed back out to the roof as well and held her so she wouldn't be scared.

Then the moment came when the door flung open, and the next hour seemed like an eternity of being in a bad nightmare with no end.

I had been sitting on the couch listening as he had driven around and around the house, too many times to count, tearing up the yard as he went, wondering if he would hit the house. The sounds ended as he ending up with one wheel on the bottom step of the side porch. I had practiced what I might say to calm him down but came up with no answers, knowing nothing would help.

As John came through the door, he was screaming the usual things, calling me names and telling me I was not a good wife, that all I cared about was the kids, and didn't care about him eating. I tried to explain his dinner was in the oven, but he wasn't interested at that point and said to blanket-blank with Halloween, and I don't remember all the details from there. It's at times like these that things happen so quickly but seems like they last forever.

I don't remember what he said to me, but everything I said just made him madder. He ran up the steps at one point and dragged my daughter down the steps and told her he would tell her what made a bad woman as he pushed her into the bathroom and closed the door as she begged, "Daddy, please," while he still screamed with rage. He said he would not let her become a bad woman (saying other words, but you can figure out what names he was saying; I'll just say "bad woman"). Then he asked her if she wanted to know what her mother and him did behind the bedroom door at night, tearing the virtue of marriage up, and saying such vulgar things I would not repeat to anyone. (My daughter was eleven at the time.) I was beating on the door till he finally opened up the door, my daughter running back upstairs and him turning to me with what always followed, the beating, till he finally got tired, calmed down, then started to cry and say he was sorry, that he didn't know what had gotten into him, then he collapsed to the floor, passing out from the liquor and drugs.

I first looked at him, crying hysterically, wanting this nightmare to go away, while a million thoughts were running through my head. I wanted out of this marriage but saw no way, but I did not want my children or myself to go through this one more night and never again.

Then I calmed down, thought to myself that there were no kids around, and my mind started working on me. John was helpless on the floor; he couldn't hurt me or the kids right now.

My thoughts ran to what I had been working on from reading the book in the library, and I saw my only opportunity to end this madness. I had been working on the idea for a while, and now was the time to take action. I ran to the screened-in back porch and retrieved the item I had been working on, and this was the moment to put the plan in action to get the job done.

This man deserved to die; he did not deserve to live. God would forgive me; it would be self-defense. I had read you could hit someone in a certain spot in the temple, and they would die instantly, but what if I missed, and he woke up? I had to take my chances and not miss. Whether or not my plan would have worked, I don't know, but I knew if it didn't, he would kill me, so I proceeded with the plan.

I crept over to where he was lying and began—at this point, he's only alive today because we have a God who's merciful and loved me too much for me to ruin my life, for He had a greater plan for me.

In an audible voice, He said, "Don't do it. I love you too much. It's not worth it. What's going to happen to your babies I gave you? They need you. I'll take care of you."

At that point, I backed off and started to cry, not fully understanding why God would allow this to happen to me, but I knew I hadn't asked God if this man was to be my husband, so why should I blame him? This was a choice I had made on my own.

Sometimes we make decisions without going to God first, and then we try to blame Him and get angry at him. He sends angels to watch and protect us but allows us to go through our mistakes so that we learn to depend on him. I've heard it said that there would not be testimonies if there weren't tests, and I believe that's true. Sometimes Jesus allows us to create our own test, as I did, but He is there all along to help us get through it.

As I composed myself, I looked at the time; what seemed like hours had only been about an hour. The time was eight-thirty. I went and gathered the kids up and told them their dad couldn't help what he did, but, "Let's just go trick or treating," anything to get away for a while.

I remember by the time we got to town for them to "trick or treat," it was actually over, and my heart went out for them. We went down a couple of blocks, and most people were rude and refused to give them candy, but a few did and blessed them with all they had that was left. But one lady actually accused them of trying to get more than their share and told them they were greedy kids and to go home; didn't they have respect for what time it was? At this house, we quit.

I pulled into a parking lot and tried to decide what to do. The kids didn't want to go home; they wanted to go to Grandma's, but I didn't feel like explaining to my family what had happened. For I knew then I would have to go through another kind of abuse, them not meaning to, but them screaming at me, asking me what was wrong within me. Didn't I have enough sense to leave him? And you know what, I didn't. I didn't realize what my options were, that my heavenly Father would take care of me if I'd just call on his name and depend on him. But I had to do it my way, and my self-worth was gone. I saw no way out and didn't want to bother anybody with my problems, and I couldn't take it anymore that night. I convinced the kids and hugged them all, trying to hug their pain away, that everything would be okay if we went home, so we did.

When we got back, I tucked all the children in bed, making sure each one knew how much I loved them and not to hate their father and to pray for him, for God loved him too. He just had problems that he needed to ask God to fix. Then I went downstairs and got a blanket and pillow and placed it under his head and covered him up.

That night, I promised myself I wouldn't ever leave God out of my conversations again. Then I went to my room and thanked Him for not letting me kill John and thanked him for me being alive to take care of my kids. I told the Lord, "You said you'd put on us no more than we could bare, but I didn't even realize what I was saying; I quoted one of my favorite Scriptures that has always carried me through, so I give it to you."

First Peter 5:7 says, "Casting the whole of your care [all your anxieties, all your worries, all your concerns, once and for all] on Him, for He cares for you affectionately and cares about you watchfully" (Amplified Bible). But we must do it, for even though I thought I was giving all to Him, I wasn't, and I have just lately begun to realize what casting all your cares on Him really means.

Are you really casting all your cares on him or just the part you are letting go of? Think about it as you continue to read this book, for this book was written to give honor to Jesus Christ and share my testimony with you to help you with what you may be going through and let you know there's hope, and it's not far away; it's one prayer away. There's a God who loves you so much that "He sent his only begotten Son, that whosoever should believe in Him should not perish but have everlasting life" (John 3:16 NKJV).

Maybe you know someone who is in a similar situation as me; don't condemn them and think you have all the answers; just love them and pray for them, or have a listening ear if they confide in you, and keep it in your heart, not in the weekly gossip.

Psalm 1 says *Selah*, which means pause and calmly think about what you just read, and then go to the next chapter because the story is not over; God has a greater plan.

CHAPTER 15

What's Growing in the Window?

I want to thank God for allowing us some good sense of humor as we are faced with life's trials. Although I have shared a lot of the trials I have encountered up to this point, I must share this story that, hopefully, brings a few moments of joy and laughter into your life. It can also let you know that even while we are going through many trials, we can still laugh and enjoy the moment.

After the Halloween incident, John spiraled out of control quickly, then quit his job and left us. I was soon told that after he left us, the police was called, and he landed in jail. His mother bailed him out, but when going to court, the judge told him he really needed to get help. Somehow, the judge was told he had a wife and seven children, and he needed to get his act together. He was fined and set free.

With no money again, I had to move, and we lived in a small city. Social Services was contacted, and a lady paid me a visit and told me John had checked himself into a rehab, and that made us eligible for help, and they helped us get a house in the city within a few days. She let me know after interviewing the kids and me that they would be by the new house and would counsel us once a week for a while.

Once again, my family stepped up to the plate and moved us in. I took all the small items, and my family moved the large items. Once we were settled in, the social worker made her first visit to the new house. She interviewed each child as well as me. That was the first time any county had gotten involved, and that was a good thing for us, for I probably would have never asked for help. She told us that John voluntarily chose to sign himself into a ninety-day drug and alcohol rehabilitation center to get help. I thought he had finally admitted he couldn't do it on his own and went without being court-ordered.

Meanwhile, I had started watering some plants that I had brought to the new house that John had been taking care of at the old house because John always grew a garden and raised good vegetables. He had always been a person who liked to grow things and had a green thumb (I never had a green thumb). So plants were always growing in our house, and this time was no different. I had watched three of the same plants that he had been growing and had noticed they seemed to grow very rapidly and didn't take much care. He had tomato plants and watermelon, among other plants that I did not know what they were, but within two weeks, most of the other plants died. I was so happy that at least three of them didn't, so I decided to place them in the house in a huge ground front window that we had in our living room. The sun would shine on them every morning, and within two or three weeks, they had grown from one foot to two feet. At this point, I started thinking maybe my green thumb was starting to work.

The social worker called and said it was time for her to come by to make her monthly visit to check up on John's progress and see how the children were doing, and she explained she needed to discuss a matter with me.

When she arrived, she interviewed the children and spoke to me, and then her subject changed. She said that everybody knows everybody in this community, and the police had asked her to talk with me about a complicated subject. She looked toward the window and said the plants looked very nice and asked me what they were. I told her I didn't know, but they had bloomed and were growing rapidly, and by now, they were almost six feet tall. I continued my conversation by telling her that this was the first time I had ever been successful in growing anything without it dying. I told her I had brought them along with other vegetables and plants that John had been raising at our other house.

The social worker's conversation continued by saying she had to speak to me about a matter the police had brought to her attention. I ask her what she was talking about, for she was beating around the bush, and I was not one to wait in suspense. She then looked at me with a pitiful half grin and laid one of her hands on top of mine, and said, "Debbie, I hate to tell you this, but those are marijuana plants." Without thinking and being in shock and embarrassed, I jumped up, ran to the window, picked up one of the plants, went to the kitchen, opened a drawer that had a small hatchet in it, got it out, ran out the back door, and axed it all up till you couldn't tell what it was. I was going to repeat the steps with each of the other two when I happened to remember the social worker was still inside, so I ran back in and sat down.

After apologizing to her, we both had a good laugh, and she told me the police would have already been here, but she assured them that I didn't know what I was growing and said she'd come out and talk with me. I excused myself from her presence to finish destroying the other two and then came back in, and we talked a few minutes more. She said she had figured they had probably been John's, and I told her they were but assured her I didn't know anything about plants, especially what marijuana looked like. To this day, I have never lived that story down, for my family jokes about it, and it's told a lot.

After the social worker left, I sat back down and thought about how serious the matter could have been. Why was I living the life I was? When were things ever going to change? I knew I had a lot to think about.

John seemed to recover pretty well. He sent letters of apologies to me and the kids and said he was forced to see how he had been treating me by watching movies that involved abuse.

John and I got back together after his stay and moved out to California. I could only say,

"California, here we come." It was a place I felt comfortable in and always wanted to be. This trip back would be the last for me except for visiting.

CHAPTER 16

Standoff at Conrad

Where does the time and years go? That's what I asked myself as I looked at the situation I was in this time. The children were older now, each in their own ways, being colder, and each taking on a new identity, not one they were born with but one that had been mapped out from their birth, only being able to change it when the time came with the help of Jesus Christ, and only then if they would or wanted to.

The time was summer, a time when the children were out of school, played extra hard, and went to bed a little later. It was a time when kids would spend more time with friends; maybe even take in some Vacation Bible School. But this certain summer is one my children would never forget. It was a summer that would change all of our lives forever.

We moved to a cul-de-sac and got to know everybody on the block. Some of our children would sometimes stay at a neighbor's house, or the neighborhood kids would come to our house.

John's rehab lasted for about six months, but soon after that, I could tell he had fallen off the wagon. He started staying up at night and said he couldn't sleep, but it would be for days at a time. Then he would finally just lay down anywhere, mostly the couch, and would sleep for a whole day. But we had to be on our tippy toes, so he wouldn't wake up because if he did, he was like the big bad wolf.

Within the last couple of years, my youngest son started having some trouble with his heart rate doubling or tripling at the drop of a hat, and suddenly he would collapse to the floor or wherever he was, and we'd have to rush him to a hospital. Nurses and doctors would quickly start working on him while I would watch and pray for him. They would finally inject some medicine into his body that would bring it down, but by then, he was weak and had to go home and rest. This was one of those days.

As John lay on the couch, one leg over the end of the couch and laying on his back with his mouth wide open, one of the boys ran into the house wanting to scream, but knowing they better not, whispered, "Mom, come quickly, Rick's having one of his heart spells again." I quickly ran out the patio doors and looked over our back fence into the school yard that was adjacent to our house and saw my son having one of many attacks that made his heart race twice as fast as it should. By now, my oldest daughter had managed to get Rick back over the fence, and I had to make a quick decision on what to do. Did I wake their dad, who had been asleep a long time, more than likely coming down from staying up two or three days, strung high on drugs, if I could get him awake, or if I did wake him up, him being very angry that I woke him up? That would have to be decided now, but Rick needed to go to the hospital. Rick had been having these spells for a long time, and they had increased his dosages over and over, but things were getting worse.

I decided to let him sleep and called my Mom who didn't live very far away. She rushed over, and we went to the hospital, and as usual, the nurses and doctors rushed us right in and started an IV with a medicine that would slow his heart down. His heart always looked like it was going to come out of his body, him lying helpless, and me knowing his life was in God's hands. We had grown accustomed to the many visits to the hospital, never knowing when Rick would have an attack. The doctors worked on a medicine that would stabilize his rate but hadn't found one yet.

Finally, the medicine started working, and after many hours, Mom took me and the children home, and I laid Rick on the bed in my room, for after the spells, he was very tired and would fall asleep.

It had now become early Friday night. Two of our boys, along with some of the neighborhood kids, had set up a tent in the backyard. They had planned on having some fun and were planning to sleep in it. Two more of our boys had gone up the street to spend the night at a neighbor's house with a couple of their friends.

After we got back from the hospital, John woke up, and we started arguing about why I had not awakened him. He said it was none of my Mom's business, and I should have woken him up. At that point, my oldest daughter, who was fifteen at the time, started arguing with him. She had gotten to the point of standing up to him. She wanted him to shut up and leave me alone. I think she hit him in the back, and then he ran after her, and she fell to the ground, and while she was down, he kicked her in the bottom of her back. To make it worse he had on steel toe work boots. I couldn't see everything that went on, for they were in the hallway, and I was in the living room. I only know it was not good to see this happening to my daughter. She had taken all she could and had chosen to lash out, maybe not in the right way, but coming to the point of not caring anymore, wanting all the violence to stop, her now being violent herself.

When it was over, things calmed down, and John ordered Melinda to go to her room, which was a big family room that came off the kitchen and had a door that went out to the garage. Melinda was now fifteen and wanting him to leave and stay gone. She had turned into a very angry young lady.

While the kids were in the back yard John and I sat in the living room, not talking but at least quiet, and Rick was asleep on our bed, and Jenny, our youngest child, lay asleep on my lap.

The next thing I knew, the front doorbell rang, and I got up to answer it. As soon as I opened the door, it seemed like police came from everywhere, pushing their way through to our living room, and John quickly sat up on the couch. I didn't know it, but policemen had stationed themselves around the entire house and were gathering up the children while back inside, two policemen and a policewoman were questioning John and me.

Melinda had snuck out the garage door and had called the police on her father for the brawl they had earlier. They questioned us on what had happened, and I tried to explain as best I could. I was scared to death. I never had a bout with the law but was used to them coming after John.

After extensive questioning, they told us they would have to take the children for the night, and we could see about getting them back the next day. I begged and pleaded with them, but nothing helped. By now, Jenny was awake and scared stiff, clinging to my skirt and holding onto me. I explained that I had never been away from my kids, and they needed me; they were my life.

John even tried to convince them to take him to jail and leave the kids with me, that I didn't deserve this, but they said they didn't have a choice; they had to take all seven children. I was crying hysterically by now, holding onto Jenny, and the policewoman tried to calm me down so they could take the kids.

Finally, Rick started crying in the bedroom, and I stood up to go get him but I was stopped, and they said they would go tend to him. I explained to them he would be scared, and I didn't want him to go into one of his spells again. I let them know he had been to the hospital that day. Thy asked where his medicine was, and I gave it to them. Jenny was still crying and holding tightly to the hem of my dress, and the woman was telling me to pull her hands off as I told them I couldn't, but she said if I didn't, she would arrest me.

After what seemed like many hours, the police became more aggressive, not wanting to, but having no choices left. I asked them if I could go with them, but they said they couldn't till they questioned all the children and got all the right facts. The policewoman became irritated and said, "Let's you and I go into another room and talk a moment." I gave Jenny to John and went in the next bedroom.

She proceeded to try her best to calm me down and said I needed to be strong for my kids and compose myself, but they had to take the children by law, and I had to let them. She told me if I didn't go back in the living room and convince Jenny to go with them, I would be arrested as well, and if I wanted that. "You have the choice to let it happen peacefully or the hard way. But if you resist, you won't get your children back right away."

At that point, I tried to calm myself and think about how to make it exciting for the children so they would go with them. I didn't want my children to be scared. As the policewoman escorted me back to the living room, I told them I'd go get Ricky, who had slept through all this, for I wanted to hold him and try to make sure he knew everything would be alright. But I was stopped and told that I couldn't leave the living room, and they had to go get him. The next thing I knew, they carried Rick out through the hallway, him looking over, trying to wake up, rubbing his eyes but not crying. Jennifer had made her way back to me, her arms tightly around my neck, not letting loose but by force, begging, "Please, Mommy, don't let them take me." I was trying not to cry and told her it would be alright and only for the night, that Mommy had to let them. I tried to comfort Jenny, but they eventually pulled her from my arms and carried her outside, screaming.

I never even got to see the rest of the children; they had gone in the backyard and talked to the boys and found out who the other children were and had gone up the street and exchanged their kids and got ours. They wouldn't even let me hug them goodbye, which I always did before they went to bed. Jenny had almost literally torn my skirt off, and I felt so helpless, so alone, more alone than I had ever known.

By now, I was a little more composed, possibly more in shock. The police had convinced me that I'd get them back in a few hours, that everything would be okay. I walked the policeman to the door, looking out and, to my amazement, seeing at least five police cruisers, not seeing my kids but knowing they were inside. I didn't cry out loud, but the tears were streaming down as I closed the door behind them.

Then I must have walked back into the living room in shock at what had just happened. There was silence. John was sitting with his face in his hands, not knowing what to say, then looked at me and started to cry, saying, "I'm sorry. I never meant for this to happen; you didn't do anything to deserve this." That was the moment that changed me from a person who had no say or voice to one who would stand up for my rights and the children's rights because I knew the battle had just begun.

After that, I don't even remember much about what happened except I went to my bedroom and cried myself to sleep. A few hours later, I woke up, and it was already Saturday at 8 a.m. I dragged myself out of bed and went to the bathroom to wash my eyes that were swollen, dry, and burning from crying so much. I reached into the pocket of my skirt and pulled out the number the police had given me to call.

I called the number and got nowhere. They said nothing could be done; it was the weekend, and nobody was in who could help me till Monday. After a few numbers I was given, I found out that social workers had been called in and had placed the children in foster care. I found out later that my babies had all fallen asleep on the floor at the police station till around two in the morning, for they were trying to keep them together but could find no shelter that could take seven kids.

The oldest child was placed in one home, the three oldest boys in another, and the youngest three were placed in another home. The older ones I knew could handle it at least on the outside, but I was scared for the younger ones. They said that on the first night, my baby girl was placed in a room by herself away from her two other brothers. She was so scared when they turned off the lights and shut her door that she went to the room where Jeremy and Rick were and went between them, and they fell asleep. The lady came in and took her out of the bed and made a statement, "Young lady, we don't sleep with boys in this house," and took her back to the other room, turned off the light, and shut the door. She was four years old.

The three youngest were moved three times in the first week, then later, because my baby girl cried so much, they moved her to where her sister was.

One day turned into a month. I was told that Monday that I had to wait until a court date was given because they couldn't release the children till then. They further explained that they were temporarily in the custody of the court.   Finally, after five days had passed and lots of phone calls, I got to talk with each one of the kids. I was told that I would be monitored and that if, at any time through the conversation, I would start crying and upset the children, or if I said I was coming to get them, the phone would be hung up. I was not allowed to know where the children were for their safety, they said. I got to talk to all of them at different times but wanting to hold them so close to let them know everything would be alright.

The older boys seemed to handle it quite well while the smaller ones didn't handle it quite the same. As they each got on the phone, saying, "Momma, you said it was going to be only one day; please come and get us," all I could say was, "It will be soon. I love you and miss you so much, and please be good for Momma."

I tried to call my oldest daughter, but she didn't want to talk to me. She was a very angry young lady. At the time, I didn't understand why, but now I understand. The anguish my children went through was horrible. The only way I can describe it is PTSD. I thought about what I was going through and how all of this affected me, but I didn't realize till years later how much pain and suffering my children went through.

As the next month passed, it felt like the longest month of my life, but the court date finally arrived. My children had been away from my arms for two and a half months. When we got to court that day, I couldn't wait to hug my kids, which was in a guarded, locked room with supervision. I felt like I was a criminal, but I knew I had never hurt any of my kids (but had I without realizing it?).

We were led by a lawyer through a hallway where the children were, my heart pounding with fear as well as with anticipation at seeing their beautiful faces for the first time since they were taken. As I walked into the room, my youngest daughter Jen looked over at the lady she lived with and asked with her eyes to get her approval to go to me. The lady smiled and said, "Honey, you can go to your mommy," and she ran and jumped into my arms with tears of joy running down both of our faces. My youngest son Rick ran the next moment, and I held them both as if there was no tomorrow.

I looked at my next youngest son, Jeremy, and he quickly came as well. For once, it seemed my arms were not long enough to extend to hold all of them. Even though Johnny, my next-to-the-oldest son walked slower, as he came close, I saw a big smile of happiness appear on his face and told me it was just good to be back by my side. My last two boys, David and Matthew, joined the already large circle, and we just passed hugs and kisses over and over. These were those precious souls that God had given me to cherish forever.

The sadness crept in when my oldest child, Melinda, chose not to see us, and they kept her in another room. As things settled, a lady came in and said we had to get ready to go into court. I asked if I could please have the children sit with me and she saw no reason why. At this point in time, you must realize that my children were four, six, eight, nine, ten, eleven, and twelve. They had been going through a war zone since their days of birth.

We all went to the hallway to a group of benches and waited till they called our names, and then we walked into the courtroom. I was very scared and silently prayed as I walked through the door. I was praying to God, "Please guide my words and actions, and please let me take my babies home today."

If you're wondering if John got to see the children, the answer is no. He was not allowed around the children or allowed to even see them. And the children did not want to see him.

There were four lawyers present, two representing the children, one representing John, and one representing me. We were advised that we had to have different lawyers to regain custody of the kids. I had no idea that on that day, the courts would rule my life and my children's for the next two years. The court proceedings lasted approximately two hours. All four of the lawyers spoke, and then they called John and I up to speak. As the testimony ended, the judge proceeded with his rulings of what had to be done.

Before the children were to be released to me, their father had to move out of the house. He was not allowed to be within five hundred yards of the children. We also had to go to parenting classes, and I had to go to Al-Anon twice a week with a signed note. I also had to seek counseling for myself once a week as well as counseling for the children and group sessions with us all. The judge stated when he saw proof, such as a rental agreement that John had moved out, then I could pick up the children from their foster homes. Once again, I had to walk away, with Jen crying and the other kids with mixed looks. The looks were somewhere between angry and heartbroken, yet not lashing out with noises, only going quietly. I'd quietly kissed them and told them it wouldn't be much longer, as their lawyers led them away back to their foster moms.

We (John and I) left as quickly as possible, not wanting to see them drive out with my babies, as well as my uncontrollable crying. John tried to comfort me, but just more of me died inside. I did not want him to touch me, look at me, or console me. At that point, it was over for me. I just wanted to get my babies back.

We drove and got a newspaper to find a place, but it wasn't easy. There were a few problems. We only had one vehicle, and that was our van. Also, we had one income. Whether I liked it or not, we had to find a place for John to live and bring the receipt back to court to get my children back. That meant letting go of our house. We finally found a room in someone's trailer for John to stay with.

Now the next problem was transportation. For once, we were discussing things without arguing, or I had some say in the subject. We discussed how we would share the van without breaking the rules as much as possible. The deal was when I needed the van, John would pull in the driveway of our home and go into the garage, and then I would load the children into the van and go do what I needed to do. He would stay in the house till we got back. Then when we'd get back, I'd go into the house, and he would go back into the garage, then the kids would get out and go into the house, then he'd leave. Now I was ready to go get my kids back.

I contacted the social worker with all the requested info and then was given the addresses of the places where the children were. I first picked up Matt, Johnny, and David, my oldest three boys, and then proceeded to get Jeremy and Ricky, the youngest two boys. The last stop was to pick up Melinda and Jenny. All of them were excited to be with me again and were happy to be going home.

Then my baby appeared and ran as fast as she could to me, and my arms were wide open to embrace her. All of my children were with me except Melinda, and we were ready to go home.

Melinda didn't want to come home, even without John there. I didn't know how to react and wasn't ready for this situation. At this point, I blamed her for my kids being taken from me, but at the same time, wanting her to know I still loved her and understood why she did it, and it was the right move, yet I didn't know how to tell her that. The words didn't come.

A week later, they called me to go pick Melinda up, and I did. She didn't hug me, but I hugged her but could feel the distance coming from her and knew that the road would be a long one for her and me.

I had to explain to all the children what was going on as far as their dad was at the house only till we got there, and then he would leave with the van. I was scared of how Melinda would react and asked her if she understood why we had to do it this way, and she nodded as if to say it was okay. When we got to the house as planned, only I went into the house, and John went to the garage through the family room door. Then the children went into the house, and John came out of the garage as we discussed our schedules, and he left. I ran inside, and at that moment, I felt that even though things were not over, I was going to make it; I had my babies back.

Once more, I must talk to you, the reader. If you or someone you know are in a similar situation like I was, seek help or talk to someone. Don't wait till the courts are dragged in. Back then, I did not see why they titled me as one of my children's abusers, but after many years, I see why they did. I did not protect my children from the abuse of my ex-husband.

Please place your life, or if you have children, your children's lives into Jesus' arms and allow Him to walk you through the situation you're in. Hope is real, and it is in our heavenly Father. He will never leave you or forsake you. Have faith in God.

CHAPTER 17
The Hideout

As weeks passed, things went pretty smooth; the schedules were very hectic but seemed to work out. There were so many appointments for me to keep up with. Life didn't end for a mother with seven children with already much to do. But then, with our situation with the van and going to therapy three times a week for the children and me, plus meetings with social services, schools, doctor appointments, lawyers, going to the store to shop for life, and it went on and on; sloppiness stepped in.

John had become a little too relaxed. He didn't try not to be seen by the children coming and going and would talk with them here and there but was not five hundred yards from the children. And the children would ask, "Can I give Dad a hug," especially the smaller ones. I didn't know what to do, for if I had addressed the problems, he would have just stayed away with the van, and I wouldn't have gone anywhere.

John was on his best behavior (just like the many times before), and I didn't realize it was happening again and bought into it. Also he and I were getting along better and since we weren't seeing much of each other, I found myself missing him (or I thought I missed him), finding out later that missing him was because I was lonely and thought I couldn't make it on my own.

I could tell Melinda was beginning to not like the idea of him being around at all. Because of what she had been put through over the past years, her anger was not going away, and she would and was capable of doing anything at any cost to keep him away, manipulating the situation at hand for her own benefit, lashing out the only way she knew how. I expressed what

I felt with him and begged him to go by the rules, but he was not one to follow many rules and didn't listen; I didn't demand that he follow the rules, and things got out of hand.

I don't remember exactly how she did it, but on a day when I needed the van, Melinda had gotten very angry at something her dad had done and somehow snuck out and called her lawyer, and her lawyer called the social workers to let them know John and I were breaking the rules. She told them John was at the house.

Then my lawyer called our house to let me know what she had done and said I better get John out of the house and I needed to go hide because the children's social workers had already met and were coming to take the kids because they had been told John was at the house, and the restraining order had been broken. My lawyer said after I got to where I was going to give him a call and tell him the whole story. I gathered up all the children except Melinda but then I remembered she had asked me if she could go to a friend's house and stay the night, and I had said yes.

At this message, the thoughts inside my head started to run wild; what was I going to do? I told John he needed to leave, and then I thought of a girlfriend who lived close by. I finished gathering up the kids, placed them in the van, and told John to drop us off a block from her house. Remember we owned only one vehicle and I told him I would contact him later to let him know what was going on. Then he drove away. My friend welcomed my children and me with open arms, but we were both very scared, waiting and watching for that moment to see the police barging in the door to take my kids away. I could not let that happen again. I was glad Melinda was gone and was safe because I couldn't let her know where we were going. I did leave a message for my lawyer to call me at my girlfriend's house as soon as he could.

I proceeded to call my mom to let her know I was okay but couldn't tell her the location of where we were because the authorities would go there first, and I didn't want her to lie. I told her to contact the social worker and let him know I would call him and explain to him what had happened, but I would not let them take my kids again without a fight.

I calmed myself down, and Lorrie, my friend, told the kids to go into the playroom to watch television as I stayed in her kitchen to call my appointed lawyer. I called my lawyer and explained in detail what I had done and ask him what I should do? But before he spoke I heard him whisper a sigh knowing I had broken the rules but at the same time understanding why I had done things like I had. He said he would contact the social worker and would get back to me. At the same time, he told me no matter what the circumstances, we had broken the law, and the judge would not like it. He proceeded to tell me that he did not know if the judge would now let me keep the kids, and I would have to turn them over because they could get me for kidnapping as well as my friend.

At that point, I was ready to run away but knew I'd had better contact the person I had left out through this whole situation (you guessed it, God, my Father, the one who had said He'd never leave nor forsake me). I started praying, asking Jesus to allow the judge to be lenient with me and have mercy to not let them take my children.

As the hours passed, my faith was not at the highest level. We (my friend and I) sat in fear, holding the smaller children; trying not to show them how scared we were but not doing a good job at it. We could see the scared little faces of theirs choosing to sit very quietly, wondering what would happen next.

Then the phone rang. Lorrie shakily moved toward the phone and answered it, then with a sigh of relief, let me know it was my lawyer. As I took the phone, he told me he had spoken to the social workers, and they had had mercy and would let the kids stay with me for the night, but we were to show up in court the next day, then he continued to say, "We'll just have to see what happens then." He told me that under no circumstances was John to bring the kids and me to court and then said good luck and hung up. What I needed was not luck but the mercy of God Himself, and only He could help me.

The next day at court, I found out the lawyer was right; the judge had no mercy and was very harsh with us. He did not care that we had only one car. He proceeded to say that the children now were to be taken out of my custody and put into the custody of the court.

One of the lawyers spoke up and asked if the children could stay with the maternal grandmother, and he agreed that would be okay as long as the children did not go back to the house. My lawyer asked if he'd have mercy on me and let me stay with my kids, and he said yes but stated that one more false move, and my children would become wards of the court, and it would be a long time before I'd get them back.

All those words sank deep in my head and my heart as I left the courtroom.

I knew in my heart things had to change. I didn't know how, but I knew they must. How was I going to do it? A million and one thoughts went through my head with my thoughts running wild. How was we both supposed to use one car? Could I make it completely on my own? How was I supposed to make sure I didn't mess up? Was my mom going to care if we all stayed in her house? Seven children and I were a lot to an already crowded three-bedroom house. Time would only tell, and all the guessing in the world would not change things.

As I approached my mom, who had been waiting outside the courtroom door, I told her what had happened, and she hugged me and said everything was going to be okay, and then we proceeded to her home.

CHAPTER 18

The Final Curtain
Must Come Down

From that moment, things got very difficult. John moved back into the house, and my house became the van located in the driveway outside my mom's house. It was like living between two homes. Mom's house was very small, so small that I had to let my older five children sleep on her living room floor, and my youngest two slept out in the van with me. We would keep the van parked right beside the house in the driveway. It was a little chilly at night, but we made it. Thank God it wasn't back east, or we would have frozen to death, but God is always in control, even when we don't realize it. While the kids were in school, I would frequently make visits to our house to wash our clothes and restock our van. This enabled me to keep plenty of clean clothes and our belongings at hand in the van as well as if John was there, then we'd talk over things that needed to be discussed. It seemed as each visit passed, we became strangers more and more.

After the first month, things got a little tiresome. It was a lot of work, but it was my job, and no one wanted it, especially John. He had created the problem but did not want to be bothered. Besides, most of the time he was at work, and we saw each other less and less.

Eventually, we seemed to move on with our lives. As time passed, I rented another house, and John took back the van and lived in it for a while. Sometimes after the kids would go to school, he would call and come by and pick me up. Then we would drive and talk, but it seemed like we never got anywhere. Each time he picked me up, the conversations got less and less. We really didn't have much in common anymore.

My life was for God and my children, and his was wrapped up in himself. He was convinced and made sure I knew none of this was his fault but Melinda's, and everything was blown out of proportion. Any time effort was involved, John would bow out. I guess his childhood had not been pleasant, and he needed much counseling but was unwilling to seek it and wanted no part of God.

The day finally came when John picked me up, and we took a drive, and then he stopped and parked on a street. He proceeded to say, "Debbie, there is no hope for us. We both need to go on with our lives. You and the kids are better off without me, and the courts are not going to let me come back." He stared at the floor as he continued to tell me that he had met someone and was staying with her and wanted me to let him go. He said he couldn't handle this life anymore and wanted things to end.

I started to cry, even though I knew there was nothing between us, and he had stated the truth. It was hard for me to be a quitter, and it seemed like that is what I'd be.

At the same time, I knew it would be the best thing that could ever happen for the children and me. We were both quiet as he drove me home for the last time we would ever be together as husband and wife. That ride was the longest ride I had ever taken. I felt in my heart that I was a failure for letting things get to this point. There must have been something I could have done or not done to make this marriage work. As he pulled into my mom's driveway, we said our goodbyes for the last time. Getting out, I was scared, brokenhearted, and lonely but, at the same time, relieved that this nightmare was over.

I stayed pretty busy for the next year due to all the things that had to be done through the court order. John and I both had to attend parenting classes, which lasted for the next twenty-two weeks. He attended a couple of the class sessions but decided right after the first two it was too much trouble and never came again, having disappeared for the next two years without any contact with me or the children or having sent any money, even on birthdays and Christmas.

The next thing on the list was that I had to go to Al-Anon twice a week and get a signed note that said I had been there. I also had to attend private counseling for myself once a week and once-a-week sessions with my children. It was not fun. I had no time for myself. It had gotten to the point where I felt I had no life and that I was in my own prison and was paying for a crime I had not been guilty of. But now I realize I was guilty of allowing them to go through what they did. It was like everyone else had his or her life but me. But I found out later throughout the years that there were many wounds for my children and me that had not healed.

John didn't have to worry about attendance because he couldn't have custody of the children anyway, and he was out of sight, nowhere to be found. The children could refuse whatever they wanted because they were minors. That left me. Either I did everything the court ordered, or they would take my children again, and I couldn't let that happen. I stuck to the rules, and the two years passed slowly, but I finally was given back full custody of my children, and we moved on.

As I look back at the state of mind I was in, I wanted to walk away from everything and never be seen again, but I stayed for my three youngest children's sake, whom I knew needed me, and I needed them.

At the time, I didn't realize the older children were lashing out any way they could, whether to get even or let go of their anger, but they needed me too. But I had so many problems of my own that I couldn't handle theirs and mine. Therefore, I didn't know how to reach them and didn't want to at the time.

As I close this story, you're probably wondering what happened in the coming years. Well, a lot has happened, but you'll have to wait for the next book, which there will be one . . . or maybe two, only God knows.

I can tell you this much; my relationship with Jesus has grown to a new level. With every decision I make, I ask Him for advice before moving forward. And the closer I get to the Savior, the more I realize He does everything His Word said He would do. And by allowing God to take control of my life, my prayers always ending with, "Not my will but yours be done," and He has given me a great, blessed life.

I will let you know this much, God did introduce me to a man five years later on in my journey, and that man said he was seeking a godly woman, and God told him I was going to be his wife. When he told me that, I told him God had already been telling me that he would be my husband; I was just waiting for him to approach me. In fact, I was starting to like someone else, and every time I prayed and asked God if he was going to be my husband, the Lord would tell me, "Ron is going to be your husband." At first, I thought, "Lord did you make a mistake?" But after three times of asking, I said "Not my will but yours be done," and God put the next steps together.

Now we have been married for thirty beautiful years to date, and we have eight children, twenty-five grandchildren, and eleven great-grandchildren so far. We have pastored a church together for the last 12 years, and the blessings just keep coming.

One final plea I ask of you right now, wherever you are; don't make your own choices, but totally depend upon God's words to direct your paths. When you choose a mate, make sure He knows Jesus Christ.

And for those of you who don't know Jesus Christ, this is the best time to receive Him into your heart right now.

Please say this prayer with me:

Jesus, I know I am a sinner, and I know you died for me and were nailed to a cross for my sins. I ask you right now to come into my heart and save me. I know you are my Redeemer, Savior, Deliverer, Healer, and Counselor. You are the one who will never leave nor forsake me. You are the best friend I could ever have, and I know you will always be the best listener I could ever have. You will not leave me or condemn me but will hold on to me. AMEN!

Whether you're young or older, please allow these words to ring into your ears: "JESUS LOVES YOU!"

He can be that father your children need. He can be your husband who will never leave. Whatever your need, He's there for you.

If this story fits your life in any way, contact someone who can help you and begin a new life free from abuse and misery.

God does not want you in that situation. He will not force you to leave, for you must make the decision on your own. But I can assure you of this, if you make a step forward and put your faith and trust in Him, He will deliver you. Make that move right now.

For those of you who have not been in this kind of relationship but know of someone who is, pray that God will give you wisdom on what to do. But please also have mercy to understand that person, for they need a true friend.

Once you are released from your abusive situation, you need to allow yourself to heal. For your healing to start, you must forgive that person. Anger is a force that eats at your soul. It can make you sick, age you before your time, and make you live a miserable life. God wants to bring joy and healing to you, but you must let go.

Instead of anger and hate, I pity my ex-husband for all the harm he has done to me, my children, and himself. The joys he has missed out on can never be replaced. But I pray for his salvation a lot and that he has sought counseling for his healing, but that lies in his hands. He must personally answer to God for himself.

I am a winner, and he is the loser. God has gotten the victory and reigns in my life.

May God bless you as you go on your way! And may this story be a blessing to your life.

Amen!

CPSIA information can be obtained
at www.ICGtesting.com
Printed in the USA
LVHW041748290323
742916LV00008B/367